The Seven Point Plan
by
Alec Rodger

New Perspectives Fifty Years On
by
Ken Rawling

NFER-NELSON

Published by The NFER-NELSON Publishing Company Ltd.,
Darville House, 2 Oxford Road East,
Windsor, Berkshire, SL4 1DF

and in the United States of America by

NFER-NELSON, 242 Cherry Street, Philadelphia, PA 19106 – 1906.
Tel: (215) 238 0939. Telex: 244489

Library of Congress Cataloging in Publication data

Rodger, Alec.
   The seven point plan: New perspectives fifty years on

   Includes text of The seven point plan.
   1. Employee selection. 2. Vocational qualifications.
I. Rawling, Ken. II. Rodger, Alec. The seven point
plan.   1985.   III. Title.
HF5549.5.S38R63   1985   658.2'112   85-15346
ISBN 0-7005-0673-X

The Seven Point Plan

First published by the National Institute of Industrial
Psychology, 1952.
Reprinted on behalf of the NIIP by the NFER Publishing
Company Ltd, 1974.
Reprinted in this edition, 1985

The Seven Point Plan: New Perspectives Fifty Years On

ISBN 0-7005-0673-X

Code 8183 02 1

Contents

The Seven Point Plan by Professor Alec Rodger is reproduced on coloured paper at the centre of the booklet.

Consultant Editor's Preface

This booklet builds on an important tradition and body of knowledge but it is also in itself an exciting and much needed addition to the literature. Selection procedures have been much -influenced by the work of the late Professor Alec Rodger and the Seven Point Plan booklet (dating back to 1952). The importance which a personnel specification is given in selection work in this country owes much to the training given to practitioners through the National Institute of Industrial Psychology, out of which the original booklet came. Successor organisations and consultants have added to our knowledge and have developed a number of selection instruments, but many governmental and private bodies and management teachers have loyally stuck to the framework which Alec Rodger created.

This loyalty can now be rewarded. The 'commentary' in this booklet remains faithful to the intentions of the Seven Point Plan, but brings together up-dated insights, knowledge and experience which will, I am sure, delight both students and practitioners. It is not easy to take a classic and do new things with it. Ken Rawling's active training work using these ideas has fitted him well for the task of writing this booklet and we are indebted to him for undertaking it.

Mac Bolton
Roffey Park Management College
February 1985

Preface to The Seven Point Plan – New Perspectives Fifty Years On

The Seven Point Plan was first written in 1930, but it was not published until 1952, when it appeared as Paper No. 1 of the National Institute of Industrial Psychology.

Although few would argue with the basic classification of human characteristics outlined in the Plan, there have been many developments and changes of emphasis since it was first conceived. Research findings in occupational psychology, new legislation and changes in social attitudes have all had ramifications for the Seven Point Plan areas. For example, the widespread use of personality questionnaires has produced much new evidence about Disposition, while current concerns about unfair discrimination have had implications for Physical Make-up and Circumstances, so much so that some have questioned the right of an employer to stipulate any requirements at all in these areas.

On the other hand, the Seven Point Plan has been so widely adopted that alterations should not be made lightly. In a sense, the Plan is the property of its many users, and they should be consulted about any proposed alterations.

NFER-NELSON has therefore decided to publish the Seven Point Plan in its original form, together with a commentary and a suggested revision of each point. The original Seven Point Plan is to be found at the centre of this booklet, and those who are new to the Plan should read this in full before moving on to the commentary, in which each point of the original Plan is appraised in the light of personnel research and recruitment practice. The proposed revision is then presented at the end of each section. These revisions constitute a 'new' Seven Point Plan which contains substantial alterations and only six points! I hope that it amounts to more than the 'private tinkering' against which Professor Rodger warned in the original version.

I should like to acknowledge the contribution made by those whose comments on the original Seven Point Plan have helped to shape the ideas presented here. In particular, the broader approach to the question of motivation which is suggested on pp.39–40 owes its origin mainly to the comments of training course parficipants.

My main acknowledgement, however, is to the work of the late Professor Alec Rodger, in whose footsteps I have had the temerity to follow.

Ken Rawling
February 1985

Introduction

The Seven Point Plan was designed as a simple but defensible assessment system for use in personnel selection and careers guidance, and is still so widely used that its value as a practical tool seems unquestionable.

Few people have suggested any major alterations to the Plan since it was first published by the National Institute of Industrial Psychology in 1952, and none of the alternatives has been so widely adopted (e.g. Munro Fraser's[1] Fivefold Framework). The popularity and resilience of the Plan is perhaps even more surprising when one remembers that it was originally devised more than fifty years ago.

One possible explanation is that the philosophy which lies behind the Seven Point Plan and the systematic approach which it encourages are just as important as its actual content. The Seven Point Plan has many ramifications, and has proved to be a highly adaptable framework for assessing people in a wide variety of situations. Some examples of its hidden agendas may help to illustrate the general approach which it encapsulates.

First let us consider its role in a systematic selection procedure. A well-designed procedure should follow at least five sequential stages:

1. **Specifying requirements**
e.g. studying the job or training programme; preparing a job description and person specification.

2. **Attracting suitable candidates**
e.g. recruitment advertising etc.

3. **Assessing candidates**
e.g. gathering and evaluating information about each applicant by means of application forms, interviews, tests and other selection techniques.

4. **Decision-making**
e.g. rejecting unsuitable applicants; selecting the most suitable candidates.

5. **Follow-up and validation**
necessary to establish reasons for any 'failures' and guidelines for future selection.

At first sight it might appear that the Seven Point Plan can only enter the picture at Stage 3, but this is not so. The Plan can be used at *every stage* in the systematic selection procedure described above. If the person specification is set out in terms of the Plan headings at Stage 1, and each candidate is assessed in terms of the same headings at Stage 3, Stage 4 should be greatly facilitated. Rejecting or selecting each candidate at Stage 4 then becomes largely a matter of comparing the Seven Point Plan assessment of the candidate from Stage 3 with the Seven Point Plan specification from Stage 1 and matching them together. At Stage 2, the essential requirements listed in the person specification form one of the bases of the recruitment advertisement. The essential requirements for a post should be specified as far as possible in the advertisement in order to reduce the number of unsuitable applications. The Plan headings can also be used to follow up selection exercises at a later date to establish how successful they have been (Stage 5).

The Seven Point Plan is also useful for building up a **total picture of an individual.** Alec Rodger quotes Oldfield's[2] notion of a 'homunculus-like representation' or 'working model', and there is much to be said for this approach. Most people working in the fields of selection and careers guidance would probably agree that building up a dynamic model of a person is preferable to describing them in terms of 'a mere bundle of "qualities"' (7PP,p.2). Those who presume to assess others would do well to remember that each individual is a unique and highly complex combination of physical attributes, abilities, personality, needs, attitudes, etc, all of which are interrelated. Attributes have to be analysed before they can be synthesised but accurate predictions about future behaviour can only be made by assessing someone as a 'whole person'. Low motivation can operate to cancel out the effects of high ability, and high motivation can compensate for limited ability. Circumstances may interact with both these attributes, producing different results in each case. A young trainee's performance will be affected by their abilities, interest pattern, motivation and enthusiasm, home circumstances, etc and by the interaction between them. All these factors (and many others) will enter into the equation. If anything, the Seven Point Plan probably understates the importance of the particular *combination* of factors operating for each individual at each point in time.

The time element brings us to another area which the Plan probably understates. Most of the seven points are attributes which are relatively permanent. A person's Attainments and past Circumstances are completely unalterable, and the other points are more or less fixed, at least for long periods of time. Alec Rodger seems to have restricted the Seven Point Plan to characteristics which a person, as it were, carries around with them. But other areas need to be assessed, most notably career aims and the motivation to work for a particular organisation, even though these are largely determined by the situation in which a person finds themself and the information available to them at any point in time. A complete assessment of a person needs to include these more variable aspects, so arguably they should be included in the Seven Point Plan framework too.

The hidden agendas of the Seven Point Plan also become apparent in the various ways in which it can be subdivided. Alec Rodger himself hints at one important subdivision when he says that the questions under the seven headings are not meant to be put directly to the applicant by the assessor, although 'It is true that some of them can be put directly in some cases, but others cannot and should not.'(7PP,p.2) It would be reasonable to ask a candidate 'What were your main responsibilities in your previous job?' It would be unreasonable to ask 'How intelligent are you?'

Margarita Mills's[3] division of the Plan into four exploration areas (Physical Make-up, Attainments, Interests and Circumstances), and three inference areas (General Intelligence, Special Aptitudes and Disposition) is the basis of her Interview Coverage Chart (shown on p.4). The four exploration areas and their subdivisions provide a useful framework for a selection or guidance interview, and remind us that the inference areas should not be covered by direct questioning. Skilled coverage of the exploration areas by a trained interviewer can provide a wealth of information, which is then used in two distinct ways:

> it may be directly relevant to the job/career path under consideration (e.g. details of health or qualifications);

> it is potentially useful for making judgements about the three inference areas (e.g. involvement in a variety of social interests may provide evidence of acceptability and influence).

FIGURE 1: AN INTERVIEW COVERAGE CHART: A SEVEN POINT PLAN BREAKDOWN

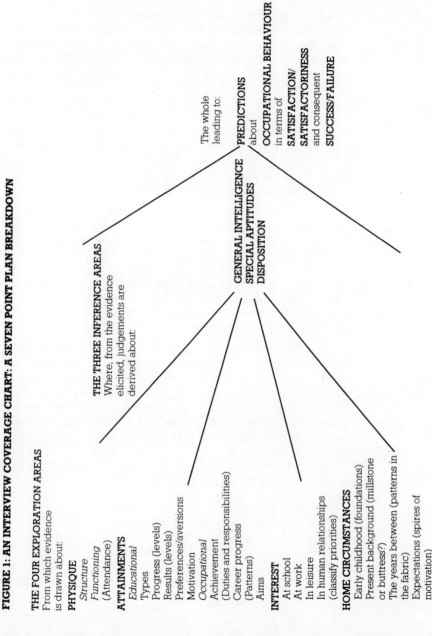

THE FOUR EXPLORATION AREAS
From which evidence
is drawn about:

PHYSIQUE
Structure
Functioning
(Attendance)

ATTAINMENTS
Educational
Types
Progress (levels)
Results (levels)
Preferences/aversions
Motivation
Occupational
Achievement
(Duties and responsibilities)
Career progress
(Patterns)
Aims

INTEREST
At school
At work
In leisure
In human relationships
(classify priorities)

HOME CIRCUMSTANCES
Early childhood (foundations)
Present background (millstone or buttress?)
The years between (patterns in the fabric)
Expectations (spires of motivation)

THE THREE INFERENCE AREAS
Where, from the evidence
elicited, judgements are
derived about:

GENERAL INTELLIGENCE
SPECIAL APTITUDES
DISPOSITION

The whole
leading to:

PREDICTIONS
about

OCCUPATIONAL BEHAVIOUR
in terms of

SATISFACTION/
SATISFACTORINESS
and consequent

SUCCESS/FAILURE

Martin Higham[4] suggested that there was a logical unity to Rodger's 'happy if hasty' compilation: 'A man's general circumstances (financial, geographical, social, etc) form his background. His idiosyncrasies, or personal characteristics, divide into his physical and psychological attributes. The former covers health, stamina, appearance, voice and physique generally; the latter splits into two main areas: the 'capacities' or talents (covering general or special abilities or skills), and the 'inclinations' or temperamental aspect (covering interests and disposition generally).'

This is an interesting 'organisation chart' of the seven points, which acknowledges their underlying logic and reminds us of the essential difference between Circumstances and the six 'internal' characteristics (Figure 2).

The Seven Point Plan has probably retained its popularity because it is a simple yet comprehensive and highly adaptable framework. Perhaps it is set out in such general terms that it is 'all things to all people'. Certainly it has become associated with a systematic, practical approach to personnel selection, and has 'made sense' to countless interviewers.

Yet in some respects the Plan reflects the thinking of the Forties and Fifties, presenting us with a rather out-of-date and incomplete picture of human attributes. Since it is essentially a practical aid rather than a psychological textbook it cannot be judged primarily from an academic standpoint, but it should not ignore research findings either. What was scientifically defensible in 1952 is not necessarily so in the 1980s. This comment applies particularly to Alec Rodger's description of Disposition, which is out of line with the bulk of personality research. If the popularity of the Seven Point Plan is to continue it must move with the times. After more than thirty years, 'the case for not changing it yet' is not quite as strong as it was — hence this commentary, and the suggested revisions which follow from it.

FIGURE 2: THE UNDERLYING UNITY OF THE SEVEN POINTS

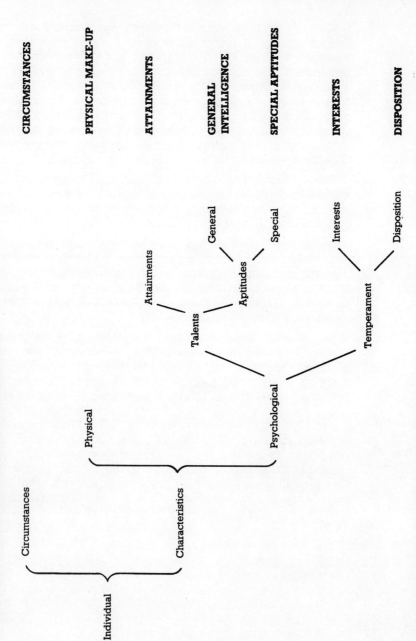

CIRCUMSTANCES

PHYSICAL MAKE-UP

ATTAINMENTS

GENERAL INTELLIGENCE

SPECIAL APTITUDES

INTERESTS

DISPOSITION

Circumstances

Physical

Attainments

General

Aptitudes

Special

Talents

Individual

Characteristics

Psychological

Interests

Temperament

Disposition

We gratefully acknowledge the Institute of Personnel Management for permission to reproduce this figure from *The ABC of Interviewing* by Martin Higham.

Assessing the Seven Point Plan Areas

The Seven Point Plan is a framework for describing the characteristics which are likely to be important in selection and guidance work. Before turning our attention to these characteristics, however, it is worth considering the techniques which are available for assessing them.

Interviewing is undoubtedly the most widely used and arguably the most flexible technique for assessing the Seven Point Plan areas. Likewise the Seven Point Plan has always had a particular significance for the interview, and has provided a most useful 'blueprint' in the form of the coverage chart shown in Figure 1. The case for the 'Seven Point Plan interview' is therefore set out in some detail below.

As Figure 1 shows, it is possible to collect direct evidence about four of the seven points during the interview, and the interview provides a means of assessing every one of the seven points, directly or indirectly.

Other methods of assessment may be required for a more detailed (and maybe more accurate) picture of specific areas of the Plan. Commercially available psychometric tests are most often used in the areas of General Intelligence and Special Aptitudes, while trainability tests are sometimes used to measure even more specific abilities. Observed discussions among small groups of candidates in a selection exercise can give information about the qualities listed under Disposition.

A complete listing of assessment techniques would include the following:

Interviews (one-to-one, joint or panel)
Tests of general ability and special aptitudes
Trainability/work sample tests
Simulation exercises
Personality questionnaires
Interest questionnaires
Application forms and letters, curricula vitae
References, testimonials, etc
Group discussions
Other techniques (e.g. handwriting analysis)

Assessment centres (which usually include most of the above, but particularly simulation exercises).

Three other titles in the Personnel Library deal separately with selection interviewing,[5] testing,[6] and trainability testing.[7]

The skills of **interviewing** tend to be seriously underrated by people who do not follow the approach illustrated in Figure 1. Some interviewers seem to think that they can accurately assess a candidate whom they have never met before by the impression they make during a half-hour interview. Often this assumption is made by managers, who are capable of using the most rigorous technical or professional skills in their everyday work, yet who, in a selection interview, seem to base their judgements on a mixture of intuition, suspicion, prejudice, whether or not they like the candidate, and so on. Afterwards, having talked of this and that, they might sum up the candidate with one of the following comments:

'He didn't come across very well'

'I found her easy to talk to'

'He impressed me'

'He seemed nervous'

'She didn't have much to say for herself '

Unless the job requires 'initial impact' skills (e.g. sales representative, airline steward) these comments are more or less irrelevant. It is notoriously difficult to assess a person's ability, personality or motivation from their reactions during an interview, and completely impossible to assess other topics such as relevant experience or availability. Candidates who appear confident and express themselves well may turn out to be insensitive and unreliable, whilst on the other hand many highly intelligent people are not particularly fluent and may appear ill-at-ease in an interview situation.

Even when these skills are required it is wrong for an interviewer to assess them purely on the basis of their own personal impressions. Interviews are somewhat contrived and artificial situations at the best of times, and people who are 'good at being interviewed' are not necessarily the most suitable, because the skills involved in being interviewed are not necessarily the same as those required in the job. To some extent the way an interviewee behaves will be determined by their understanding of the *role* they are expected to play. Do they think the interviewer wants them to be aggressive or deferential? To be full of enthusiasm or cool and rational about the job? To ask detailed questions about conditions of service, or not to mention them? Herriot (1981)[8] describes the selection interview as 'a rule-governed social interaction with clearly defined reciprocal roles allocated to both parties' but says that 'there is always the possibility of behaviour which is outside role expectations'. He describes three sets of conditions which may be in operation:

1. Interviewers and interviewees may **agree** or **disagree** about their respective roles in the interview;

2. the behaviour on which the candidate is assessed may be **in-role** or **out-of-role**;

3. interviewers may attribute personality characteristics to candidates **rationally** or **irrationally.**

Interviewers are more likely to draw rational conclusions about personality from behaviour which would not normally be expected from the interviewee's role, i.e. from behaviour which is **out-of-role.** When they base their conclusions on behaviour which is only to be expected from the interviewee's role in the interview they are probably attributing personality characteristics irrationally. Interviewers will be able to make accurate assessment of Disposition only when there is a **mutual understanding of roles** and conclusions about Disposition are drawn **rationally** from behaviour which is **out-of-role.**

Role expectation is not the only factor which influences an interviewer's reaction. The interviewer's own behaviour will also have an affect. It is interesting to observe the same person being interviewed consecutively by three or four different interviewers. Although some of the variation in the interviewee's answers and reactions from one interview to the next can be accounted for in terms of increasing confidence and 'warm-up', a somewhat different picture is displayed on each occasion. An interviewer's nervousness or confidence can be reflected in the reaction of the interviewee to a remarkable extent.

With complex factors like these in operation it is hardly surprising that interviewers who concentrate on behaviour rather than evidence draw so many unjustified conclusions and often arrive at quite different conclusions about the same candidate. In a well-known study by Hollingworth[9] twelve sales managers interviewed fifty-seven candidates for jobs as sales representatives. When the candidates were ranked in terms of overall suitability every candidate received a wide range of rankings (although this may also simply reflect the fact that the interviewers were not using a standard approach).

Other studies have confirmed the low reliability and validity of the selection interview. Ulrich and Trumbo[10] carried out a comprehensive survey of research into selection interviewing. One of their general conclusions was that it is very difficult to separate the contribution made by the interview to selection decisions from that provided by application forms, tests, etc. Although most of the studies which they reviewed reported low reliability and validity coefficients, systematic, planned interviews seemed to be more successful than unsystematic ones, and assessments of personal relationships and motivation to work seemed to provide the most accurate predictions. More recent studies have tended to confirm these findings.

Almost by definition, a **biographical approach** is needed in any interview which aims to provide a Seven Point Plan assessment. The distinguishing feature of this approach is that it is primarily concerned with evidence about the candidate obtained *from* the interview rather than with the candidate's behaviour *during* the interview. Of course behaviour is not ignored altogether. But subjective impressions, intuition, and other reactions to the candidate should be supported by evidence from outside the interview if at all possible. It is not enough to conclude that a candidate is acceptable to others because you liked them; you should try to find indications from job history, leisure interests etc to back up this hypothesis. If you find their manner impressive, how does this impression square with their actual achievements? Even health can be approached in the same way. The candidate may look fit and healthy, but are they? How much time have they had off work during the last couple of years, and for what reasons?

A biographical interview can provide a much more reliable and accurate assessment than any attempt to judge a candidate by the impression they make or the way they behave during the interview. It also has the advantage of flexibility – questions can be tailored to take advantage of the information already available about each candidate, and areas which are highly relevant or about which little is already known can be probed in considerable depth. The Interview Coverage Chart should help to ensure that all the exploration areas are comprehensively covered. The breadth and depth of coverage and the need to make the most efficient use of information already available mean that this type of interview needs to be systematic and planned.

Physical Make-up

At first sight there appears to be little to add to Alec Rodger's analysis of this area. Few would quarrel with the general breakdown into **health/physique** and the 'first impression' areas of **appearance, bearing,** and **speech.**

However, a further separation between physique and health – in other words, between bodily **structure** and **functioning** – is useful in practice. 'Structure' refers to all those characteristics which are more or less fixed, such as age, sex, height, weight and general body-build. The extent to which a person's body is in good working order is considered under 'functioning', which includes considerations of health, vision, hearing, strength and disability.

There may be special job requirements under either heading. Although good general health is essential for almost any employment, some jobs have particular requirements in terms of physique (e.g. police officer, jockey) whilst others require particular aspects of functioning to be better than normal. In some cases a job could not be carried out by someone who is physically disabled (e.g. building worker) or colour-blind, although the importance of deficiencies in structure or functioning can be over-emphasised. There are some notable examples of jobs being successfully filled by disabled people, or those with a sensory deficiency. There are telephone switchboard operators who are registered blind, and many colour-blind printers and electricians.

In the interests of precision it seems sensible to consider structure and functioning separately, to express requirements under these two headings positively rather than negatively, and to be as specific as possible.

Perhaps **physical impact** would be the best way of describing the third area of Physical Make-up which includes such attributes as appearance, bearing and speech. Munro Fraser called these attributes 'impact on others', but this description is not entirely satisfactory because it could equally well refer to personality characteristics.

It is most important to distinguish personality from physical attributes, or unfair discrimination will indeed have occurred. It may be necessary to assess appearance and speech in cases where these characteristics are considered to be relevant, as they are in most occupations involving direct contact with the general public or with an organisation's clients. Self-fulfilling prophecies apart, however, no relationship has ever been established between physical impact and personality. Nor can we draw any firm conclusions about a person's personality from their general physique. Sheldon[11] developed a procedure for describing body-build in terms of three components – in simple terms, fatness, muscularity and linearity – and claimed that each component was associated with a particular aspect of temperament. However, these results were not replicated elsewhere, and the relationship between body-build and personality appears to be far too weak to allow accurate predictions to be made in individual cases.[12] It therefore seems quite wrong to infer personality characteristics from *any* aspect of Physical Make-up.

Unfortunately, this is exactly what does happen in many selection situations. Despite the absence of any evidence that Physical Make-up indicates personality, research has frequently shown that physical attractiveness, posture, mannerisms and speech all have a considerable effect on interviewers' judgements.

Posture and mannerisms have been shown to be related to selection interview outcomes. Successful candidates in a panel interview look at the interviewers more frequently, smile more, and shake or nod their heads more than unsuccessful ones (Forbes and Jackson, 1980).[13]

There is some evidence that sex differences between candidates and/or interviewers affect interview judgements, although Elliott (1981)[14] found no overall differences in interview decisions between male and female interviewers or candidates in a study of interviewing procedures in an Irish bank.

Professor Honey considers that in some respects the prejudices surrounding accents have been getting stronger. Recent research suggests that qualities such as honesty, integrity, intelligence, ambition and even – we have come full circle – good looks are attributed to unseen speakers who speak RP – 'Received Pronunciation' – the technical term for what might best be described as 'BBC English'. 'Beneath RP, other British accents then constitute a hierarchy in descending order, with Edinburgh Scottish high on the scale, going down through Geordie and Yorkshire and West Country until we find four accents competing for rock-bottom place in popular esteem.[15]

A person's socio-economic status probably can be inferred with some degree of accuracy from their speech, but in selecting someone for a job we should not be in the business of judging people according to their membership of a category. We often have to make probabilistic judgements in selection and guidance, but these **judgements should be based on a person's individual characteristics and their combined effects.**

There are three basic assessment errors which seem to apply particularly to physical impact:

1. Making assumptions.
2. Ipsative errors.
An ipsative error results from the attribution of a characteristic to a person because they possess another characteristic, e.g. assuming that an articulate candidate is intelligent. There are two particular types of ipsative error which should be noted:

    i. **normative errors** – attributing a characteristic to a person because they are a member of a particular class or group, e.g. assuming that a candidate from a minority ethnic group will automatically have a poor command of English.

    ii. **holistic errors** (the halo/horn effect) - forming an overall impression from one or two outstandingly good/bad characteristics, e.g. being more favourably disposed to someone who is very good-looking, or biased against someone with a strong regional accent.

3. Primacy.
This is the tendency to make interview judgements on the basis of first impressions, whether good or bad (they never seem to be indifferent) and for everything that subsequently occurs to reinforce the initial judgement. There is evidence that first impressions are quickly reinforced by further supporting information, but very resistant to change in the face of information to the contrary.[16] We hate uncertainty, and aim to reduce it by pigeonholing people as quickly as possible. We are also far too susceptible to charm.

Ipsative errors, assumptions and primacy can result in disastrous selection decisions and lead to unfair discrimination.

The Seven Point Plan has another implicit message, with particular relevance to physical impact:

consider each person as an individual;

consider each of a person's attributes separately at first;

always try to support judgements by evidence.

Since the tendency to be influenced by physical impact is apparently so strong, interviewers should go to great lengths to resist it. Physical attributes of any kind should only be given weight if the job requires them, and other characteristics should not be inferred from them.

What, then, should we be trying to assess in the area of physical impact, when all these strictures have been observed?

Appearance encompasses all visible features, i.e. visible physique, hair/eye colour, facial features and dress, although, as Alec Rodger puts it, 'a remediable carelessness or eccentricity of dress is to be given less weight, in the assessment of appearance, than markedly unprepossessing physique or lack of "good looks"!' (7PP,p.6)

Bearing has always caused the most difficulty. It is a word which is incomprehensible to many people nowadays, and Alec Rodger himself seems to have used it rather loosely. 'In the assessment of bearing', he says, 'consideration is to be given to smartness and vigour ....' (7PP,p.6) – thus immediately confusing it with both an aspect of dress and a personality characteristic.

Unfortunately there is no single word to describe the effect which a person's physical presence has on others. It seems better to continue to use the word 'bearing', but to try to define it more clearly, with a little help from *Roget's Thesaurus*, as, say:

carriage
charisma
demeanour
deportment
posture

The concept also becomes more meaningful when used with an adjective. If we say that someone had an 'impressive bearing' or 'an authoritative manner' our meaning is usually clear.

Speech is much easier to define and describe. Only the physical qualities of speech should be considered under this point: loudness, pitch, clarity, pronunciation and type/degree of accent. Fluency and use of vocabulary are better considered under Special Aptitudes.

There is less to Physical Make-up than meets the eye!

PHYSICAL CHARACTERISTICS

Structure

Age	Reach
Sex	Left/right handedness
Height	Disabilities
Weight	Body-build

Functioning

General health record	Vision – Acuity
(past and present)	– Colour vision
Illnesses	Hearing
Accidents	Sense of smell
Allergies	Sense of taste
Phobias (e.g. fear of flying)	Sense of touch

Physical Impact
Appearance
Bearing
Speech: loudness/pitch/clarity/pronunciation/accent

Attainments

Attainments is an uncontroversial and self-evident area of the Seven Point Plan, although it requires extensive coverage and usually occupies the greater part of a selection interview. Unfortunately it is also the area in which least guidance can be given to selectors.

There is a clear distinction between Attainments and (mental) abilities. **Attainments are knowledge and skills already learned, whereas abilities are potential for learning.** The chronological details of a person's qualifications and career history are also included under the heading of Attainments.

The distinction between Attainments and abilities is rather like the distinction between computer software and hardware. The term 'software' refers to programs and data held in a computer's memory or storage system, just as Attainments refers to a person's experience, knowledge and skills, also stored in memory. 'Hardware' refers to the technical specifications and capabilities of an information technology system, just as a description of human mental abilities refers to capabilities for learning and processing different kinds of information.

The distinction is sometimes overlooked in describing the attributes required for a particular kind of work. The following example is a list of the most important 'skills' which a company considered were needed by its senior managers:

Interpersonal skills	Technical competence
Control skills	Ability with words
Initiative	Creativity
Ability to adapt to new technology	Persistence
Flexibility	Numeracy
Communication skills	Presentational skills

It is misleading to describe all these characteristics as 'skills', i.e. Attainments. Some of them are Attainments (e.g. technical competence), but some are abilities (e.g. ability with words); some are dispositional characteristics (e.g. initiative) and some are a mixture. Some would be difficult to assess and some obviously overlap. The framework provided by the Plan helps us to define personnel requirements more sharply than this, and to think more clearly about what can or cannot be changed.

Educational Attainments

Alec Rodger's original headings need to be added to rather than altered in this area, to remind us that candidates from different age groups will have a variety of educational experience and qualifications. For example, where he refers to 'secondary grammar, secondary technical or secondary modern' we need to add comprehensive and bilateral schools; and CSE and other 16 plus examinations need to be mentioned alongside 'General Certificate of Education/School Certificate'. Perhaps less emphasis should be given to comparisons with other people and more stress laid on the need to assess knowledge and skills relevant to employment.

Most people can see the relevance of investigating job-related further education qualifications, but some question the need to ask adults about their schooldays. The arguments for doing so should be obvious: school attainments *are* relevant in assessing young adults, particularly for sponsorship on BTEC or other further education courses; better predictions can be made by taking the long view; and, above all, it will not be possible to discover anything significant about a person's schooldays unless they are covered. Just as it is better to carry out a pre-flight check on a jumbo jet than experience engine failure at 30,000 feet, on a lesser scale it is better to check out an interviewee's school record than to disregard it and then subsequently discover that the new recruit has the wrong 'A'-level grades, or was the school arsonist. Admittedly the relevance of school attainments declines with age. But, even with older candidates, a brief discussion of the school period can sometimes shed light on other areas or help to explain attitudes. And notable achievements at school can put a different perspective on later successes (or lack of them).

The educational system

Since every practitioner needs to have some understanding of the educational system, a brief summary is presented in the following paragraphs. It has changed a great deal since the Plan was first published, and those who encounter candidates drawn from a variety of age groups also need to know some history. When the Seven Point Plan was first published in 1952, the basic structure of state schools was as follows:

Primary schools   - infant schools (5–7)
                  - junior schools (7–11)

Allocation to different types of secondary school was based on the 11-plus examination, which was compulsory, as follows:

Secondary modern schools (11–15; in some cases 11–18)
Technical schools (11–18)
Grammar/high schools(11–18)
        OR
Bilateral and Comprehensive Schools, which combined two or three of the above schools

Local education authorities (LEAs) also paid the fees of pupils from state primary schools who were offered places at the direct grant grammar schools.

Today there are still remnants of these systems, although most local authorities are now fully comprehensive. Within the present system of comprehensive education there are, however, a number of variations (see Figure 3). LEAs may adopt the type of system which they consider to be best suited to their area, provided that their plans have been approved by the central education authority for England and Wales (currently the Department of Education and Science). Comprehensive schools have had a longer history in Scotland, where pupils normally transfer from primary to secondary schools at the age of twelve.

Special schools exist for the physically or mentally handicapped and for maladjusted children, but there are also schools for children with special abilities; they are either run by the LEAs or are independent. Many ordinary schools also provide special classes or individual tuition.

Outside the state system, independent or private sector schools are fee-paying and receive no financial support from the State. The direct grant grammar schools (which have now been phased out) used to offer at least twenty-five per cent of their places to pupils from state primary schools. Some independent schools still take pupils whose fees are paid by means of a scholarship or, in exceptional cases, by their LEA.

Within the private sector, there are several types of independent schools. Most of the direct grant grammar schools have

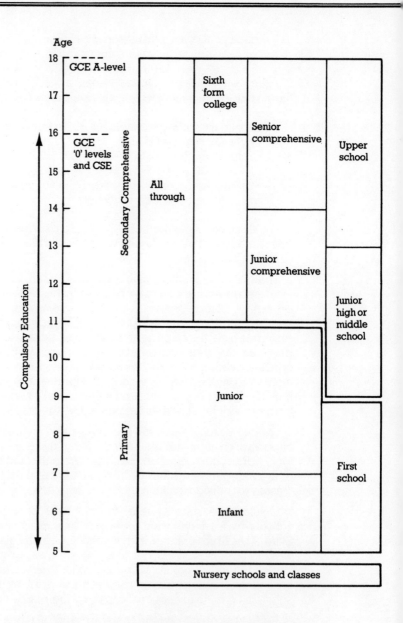

**FIGURE 3: STATE EDUCATION IN ENGLAND AND WALES
THE MAIN TYPES OF SYSTEM**

become fully independent. The public schools are part of the private sector – they are usually run by a board of governors or council and their headmasters are members of the Headmasters' Conference. Private schools are generally run by an individual or trust for private gain. A traditional but still common system is:

Kindergarten/nursery schools/play groups (3–5)
Pre-preparatory schools (5–7)
Preparatory schools (7–13)
Independent secondary schools such as the independent grammar schools, public schools, private secondary schools (13–18)

Not all the independent schools are selective, but entry to the public schools is generally by means of the Common Entrance Examination (usually taken at 13). This examination is set by the Board of Managers, but individual schools mark the examination papers and decide their own pass mark.

Further/higher education has also undergone radical changes, but fortunately those involved in selection usually only need to be acquainted with those aspects of the further education system which relate to their area of specialisation. There is some confusion, incidentally, in everyday use between the terms further and higher education, but generally speaking further education (FE) refers to all education after school-leaving age (the minimum school-leaving age was raised from 15 to 16 in 1972); whilst higher education refers specifically to institutions which award degrees – universities, polytechnics and colleges of higher education.

Examinations

The examination system has altered along with the changes in school organisation. Practitioners might well encounter people who took GCE examinations when the grading system was different. A candidate in their fifties might even have a School Certificate rather than GCEs.

A **School Certificate** could be gained only by passing examinations in at least five subjects taken at the same time, the subjects being chosen from three groups. Higher School Certificate was awarded for pupils who obtained credits in three 'main' subjects, or in two main subjects and two subsidiary subjects (or main passes), all taken at the same time.

The **General Certificate of Education** (GCE) was introduced in 1951 to replace the General and Higher School Certificate. GCE examinations may be taken one at a time, at either Ordinary or Advanced level ('O' level or 'A' level), and under one of eight separate examining boards, all of which are connected directly or indirectly to universities. 'O' levels, normally taken at age sixteen, are widely accepted as the entry qualification to many types of employment and further education. 'A' levels in two or three chosen subjects are normally taken at eighteen. A minimum of two 'A'-level passes is required for university entry, and 'A'-levels provide exemption from the preliminary examinations of many professional bodies. The table below summarises the different grading systems which have been used for 'O'-level examinations at different times and by different examining bodies.

Approximate Comparison of GCE 'O'-Level Grades

Grades in each subject prior to 1975:			From 1975 all boards have adopted the following system:	
75 – 100	1	A	Every candidate whose	A
70 – 74	2	B	performance is regarded as	
60 – 69	3	C	being of a sufficient	B
55 – 59	4	D	standard to be graded is	
50 – 54	5	E	awarded a certificate	C
45* – 49	6*	0*		
42 – 44	7	F	but these grades are	D
35 – 41	8	G	below the entry standard	E
0 – 34	9	H	required by many further education bodies	ungraded

* 'O'-level pass standard prior to 1975

Formerly, 'A'-level passes were graded from A to E; candidates whose performance was below the standard required for an 'A'-level pass were awarded grade O ('O'-level pass standard); those whose performance did not meet even this standard were awarded grade F (fail).

Currently, 'A'-level passes are still graded from A to E, but candidates whose performance is below the standard required for an 'A'-level pass are now awarded an 'O'-level grade.

There is only one examining board for the **Scottish Certificate of Education** (SCE), which is offered at Ordinary and Higher grade ('O'- and 'H'-grade), and replaces the former Scottish Higher Leaving Certificate (SHLC) with its 'Lowers' and 'Highers'. 'O'- and 'A'-level papers are also sometimes taken in Scotland.

The **Certificate of Secondary Education** (CSE) was introduced in 1965. It is more broadly-based than GCE 'O' Level and has never been a pass/fail examination – pupils are awarded a grade from 1 to 5, or are ungraded, in each subject. Grade 1 CSE gives the same qualification as 'O'-Level Grade C for entry to some courses. The CSE examinations are organised by fourteen regional examining bodies but it is important to remember that there are three different 'modes' for CSE syllabuses and examinations, as follows:

Mode 1 –syllabus and examinations devised by the examining body

Mode 2 –syllabus devised by a school or group of schools but examined by the examining body

Mode 3 –syllabus and examinations devised and marked by schools

CSE examinations are not taken in Scotland.

At the time of writing (Summer 1984) the Scottish examination system is in the process of being altered again, and proposals for a unified General Certificate of Secondary Education for England and Wales have just been announced.

Occupational attainments

Little is said in the Plan about occupational attainments, arguably the most important and relevant area in any assessment of an adult. Alec Rodger stresses the need for comprehensive coverage on page 7, but unfortunately provides no further guidance about the areas to be covered.

In effect, coverage of occupational attainments needs to consist of a series of miniature job study interviews, each covering a particular job (or group of jobs within the same organisation). The same kind of information is needed as is required to draw up a job description, although of course in much less detail. Only in this way can the assessor find 'the clues....in this individual's occupational record that will help me to make a really satisfactory prediction of his suitability for the work I have in mind for him'. (7PP,p.7)

The checklist below is not intended to be used in every situation, although the main duties, responsibilities and accountabilities will usually need to be established. By listing all the topics which *might* need to be considered, however, it attempts to go beyond the brief suggestions given in the original Plan. Interviewers certainly have their work cut out to assess occupational attainments with any degree of accuracy.

ATTAINMENTS

Educational Attainments

General education

Type (comprehensive, independent, etc)
Level   ('O'- or 'A'-level GCE, degree, etc)
Qualifications ('O'- or 'A'-level GCE, degree, etc)
Languages or specially important subjects

Specific training

Apprenticeship, City & Guilds, BTEC, RSA, other special or commercial qualifications; professional qualifications.
Stage of membership of trade or professional associations
Length of training period
Structure of training (full-time, block/day release etc)

Occupational Attainments

For each job or group of jobs:

Job title, department, organisation
Position in hierarchy (to whom responsible, number of 'subordinates')
Main duties (tasks, activities, time breakdown)

Main responsibilities or inputs:

> people (number, level, frequency of supervision)
> money (amount, budgetary procedures)
> equipment (type, value, nature of responsibility)
> materials (type, quantity, value, nature of responsibility)
> information (type, accessibility, confidentiality)

Main accountabilities or outputs; what results and what standards of performance are required from the job holder in:

> policy-making (in what areas, to what extent)
> objective/target setting, deadline setting/meeting, timekeeping
> organising, managing or supervising to achieve objectives
> reviewing, monitoring or controlling
> developing new ideas or products
> developing/training people
> other (e.g. marketing/selling, promoting or maintaining organisational image, safety)

Relationships within and outside the organisation (type, level, frequency and number of contacts)
Judgement (degree of judgement/autonomy, and its consequences)
Other relevant aspects (e.g. physical and social working environment, travel, remuneration, etc)

General Intelligence and Special Aptitudes

Unfortunately these two areas of the Seven Point Plan are neither self-evident nor uncontroversial. Their description in the Plan is based on a particular theory of mental abilities – Vernon's[17] hierarchical group factor theory – which was predominant in Britain in the 1950s.

This theory provides a comprehensive description of human mental abilities (Figure 4). The important thing to remember about the hierarchy diagram is that it is rather like an organisation chart: it does *not* represent a breakdown of General Intelligence into its component parts. The more specialised abilities lower down the hierarchy are conceived as being separate from General Intelligence, not subdivisions of it.

In the hierarchy theory, General Intelligence ('g') is represented as the apex of the organisation chart in the role of chief executive, with two powerful 'heads of department' underneath: verbal–educational ability (v:ed) and spatial–mechanical ability (k:m). The middle and junior managers in this system – the minor group factors – would include the Special Aptitudes listed in the Seven Point Plan. The hierarchy diagram suggests that it is also possible to identify more specialised abilities at these levels (e.g. fluency with words, ability to understand word meanings, and ability to comprehend verbally presented information might be identified as three more specialised areas of verbal ability). At the bottom of the diagram are the most basic units of ability, too numerous to be separately identified.

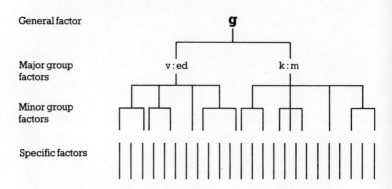

General factor

Major group factors

Minor group factors

Specific factors

FIGURE 4: THE HIERARCHICAL STRUCTURE OF HUMAN ABILITIES (FROM VERNON[17])

The Seven Point Plan

Alec Rodger

Its Aim and Nature

Many of us are often faced with the task of summing up the employment potentialities of other people. Frequently, perhaps, we have to consider the suitability of a candidate for a certain vacancy. Occasionally, maybe, we have to give somebody advice about his career. The Seven Point Plan is meant to help us to do such jobs as these in a competent fashion. It aims at providing us with a simple but scientifically-defensible assessment 'system'.

The plan consists of a series of questions gathered together under seven headings. It should be regarded as a short list of items that seem to deserve consideration in any comprehensive investigation of a person's occupational assets and liabilities. As we shall see later, the items have been chosen for their general usefulness.

In order that the reader may be able to keep his eye on the plan's headings and questions as he goes through this text, they have been printed on the final page. But before he studies them in detail he should have his attention drawn to some of the limitations of the scheme as a whole, and to certain other relevant matters.

Some of its Limitations

First let us note that the plan is not put forward as the only reasonable assessment system for employment purposes. It is not even claimed that it is an exceptionally good one. There are others with similar aims and similar contents, including the schedule produced by Sir Cyril Burt[3] from which the present scheme was derived in the years between the wars. But the Seven Point Plan seems to have an advantage over most others, in that experience has shown it to be a popular 'utility' article. There is evidence that it is being used for many assessment purposes by many people in many places.[8, 9, 21]

1

Secondly, we must not let the apparent tidiness of the plan tempt us into imagining that the device of splitting a person's attributes and circumstances into seven 'segments' is anything better than a rather regrettable necessity. The divisions we make are for convenience. We must freely admit that a shortcoming of any scheme of this sort is to be found in the fact that it may encourage us to think of an individual as a mere bundle of 'qualities'. Of course, this is not an argument for disdaining the use of such a plan: it is an argument for using it sensibly.

Nor, thirdly, must we allow its cross-sectional pattern to blind us, even momentarily, to the fact that everyone's attributes and circumstances are continuously changing. It is particularly important that we should remember this when we are summing up young workers and school-leavers. Accordingly, we must do our best, despite the difficulty of the task, to see them not only as they are now but also as they have been in the past. In no other way can we judge the trends of their development; and in all employment interviewing the appreciation of such trends is necessary, for the simple reason that our problem is essentially one of forecasting.

Fourthly, we must recognise that neither the Seven Point Plan nor any other is likely to turn a bad judge of people into a good one. Thoughtful and frequent use of it may make him less bad than he was before, but beyond that it cannot be expected to take him. On the other hand, although it may seem of doubtful value to a person who is already a good judge, possibly even he may gain a little from occasional reflection on its contents. They may perhaps remind him of the danger of neglecting what is more important than he sometimes imagines, or of emphasising things that may not really matter very much.

It must also be understood that the order in which the headings appear is not meant to carry any implications whatever about the order of their importance. The weight to be attached to a particular heading, or to a particular item under a heading, will depend to a considerable extent on the nature of the employment or training for which an applicant is being considered, and on the nature of the other information assembled about him.

It is not intended that any attempt should be made to deal with the seven sections of the plan in the order in which they appear on the paper. We must be ready to take our facts, and to form our opinions, as opportunity offers, after the manner of a sorter in a post office. We must do our mental pigeon-holing, with our seven 'boxes' in front of us, while we are interviewing, while we are studying application forms, reports and testimonials, while we are talking to people who know the applicant, and indeed at any other convenient time.

Finally, it must be realised that the questions under the seven headings are not meant to be put directly to the applicant by his assessor. They are questions for the assessor to ask himself about the applicant. It is true that some of them can be put directly in some cases, but others cannot and should not. In general, they are to be regarded as queries for the guidance of the questioner. It is safe to say incidentally that the questioner who, in the interview situation, keeps them all firmly in mind is not likely to be greatly troubled by the unmethodical assessor's problem: What shall I ask him next?

Homunculus Oldfieldianus

An idea of substantial value to the user of the plan, both as a supplement to it and as a reminder of the second and third limitations already noted, has been outlined by Oldfield.[12] 'The interviewer after the interview (and in general any person after an encounter with another) possesses and carries about with him a kind of homunculus-like representation of the candidate. This is essentially a "working model", a "living image"; and when occasion demands it can, so to speak, be taken out of its box and be made to perform. It is by placing this creature in imagined circumstances, and watching its behaviour, that the interviewer is enabled to make predictions about the candidate's probable behaviour in those circumstances.'

He adds: 'The homunculus . . . is essentially a "going concern" . . . (It) is not constructed as a corpse in the first instance, and then later infused with the breath of life'. Nevertheless, as Wilson[24] has indicated, in the building up of his working model the assessor can very profitably employ headings of the sort used in the Seven Point Plan. Oldfield's notion is, of course, a useful extension of the thought in many people's minds when they say, for example, I can't see him doing that, or, I can easily picture him being very good at so-and-so.

Crucial Activities and Situations

We can go even farther, and argue[15, 19] that in assembling our knowledge of an occupation for personnel selection or vocational guidance purposes we should aim primarily at having at our disposal, in our mind's eye, a series of pictures of the activities and situations involved in that occupation. As we construct our working model of the applicant with the aid of the Seven Point Plan, we can pitch into one activity after another, and one situation after another, and observe its performance. And if we accept what has already been said in this pamphlet about the importance of studying successes and failures, we shall, in fashioning our pictures, pay special attention to the activities and situations that appear to be crucial, in that those who fail in them are likely to become (as the Americans say) 'separated' from the occupation.[7, 16]

There are, of course, some differences to be observed in the application of this notion to a personnel selection problem and its application to vocational guidance. For instance, in dealing with the former we may be able to make use of a set of fairly specific occupational 'pictures', derived from a detailed study of the work which will in fact have to be done by the chosen applicant. In dealing with the latter, at least in the early stages of the formulation of our advice, we shall have to think for example, not of a particular clerical post but of work of a clerical 'type'.

This is one of the main reasons why the problems of the vocational adviser are often trickier than those of the personnel selector. Associated with it is the much greater difficulty the vocational adviser experiences in making allowances for his inability to judge how well a person will 'fit in' with the people with whom he will in fact have to work. But once again we have to note that the snags created by unknown factors of this kind do not provide us with an excuse for being casual about the relatively known factors which can be taken into account.

3

The Case For Not Changing It Yet (1952)

These and other limitations of the plan have led some users of it to suggest changes – the addition of a question here, the omission of one there, the alteration of the wording of several, and perhaps even the recasting of the whole scheme. A number of their proposals seem to have had considerable merit. The system as it stands is admittedly far from perfect, even within its acknowledged limitations, and it would be surprising if valuable critical and constructive comments were not sometimes made about it. But the potential improver of the plan must realise that changes – piecemeal, local, temporary changes particularly – carry important disadvantages as well as possible advantages.

In the first place, it is only by close adherence to the plan as it stands that we can benefit properly from the experience of other people who use it. Let us consider the use of the system in the investigation of the 'requirements' of occupations. Such investigation is needed in both personnel selection and vocational guidance, for both involve the matching of people and work. Now, if the matching is to be done satisfactorily, the requirements of an occupation must be described in the same terms as the attributes of the people who are being considered for it. Suppose, then, that we privately alter the Seven Point Plan: what happens? The chief result is that we are unable to make full use of information about occupational requirements that has been collected by others who have adopted the scheme in its existing form.

But there is a more fundamental – and more technical – reason for leaving the plan alone. It springs from the fact that our object in devising an arrangement of this kind at all is to have at our disposal a generally-useful system based on scientific enquiry into the attributes and circumstances that most commonly influence occupational success and failure. Indeed, we are seeking to compile a short-list of 'influences' (or 'conditions', or 'determinants') which, in our personnel selection and vocational guidance activities particularly, we shall neglect at our peril, because thorough enquiry has shown them to be the most generally important.

This means that our listed items in our Seven Point Plan should conform to four criteria. (1) They should be relevant, in that they should pin-point influences commonly and demonstrably connected with occupational success and failure. (2) They should be independent in that they should be sufficiently separable from one another to enable us to avoid overlapping assessments that would be wasteful. (3) They should be assessable in the circumstances in which the assessments have usually to be made. (4) They should be few enough to keep the risk of hasty, superficial judgement to a minimum but numerous enough to cover the ground adequately.

It follows from this that what is needed for the improvement of the plan is not private tinkering but a series of substantial researches directed to four ends. First must come the clarification of our ideas about the nature of occupational success and failure. Secondly, we must identify, according to these ideas, groups of successes and failures in occupations of different types and levels. Thirdly, there must be a detailed comparative study of these groups of successes and failures, which will take account of all manner of information about their attributes and circumstances, and will 'quantify' it appropriately, in order to make it amenable to statistical treatment. Fourthly will come the statistical analysis of the data thus obtained, which will have the object of isolating the chief influences we are looking for, and learning how to describe and assess them in such a way that we shall be better able than we are now to forecast success and failure.

However, it is not inconsistent with this argument to say that there can be no objection to the addition of items to the standard list, where this seems desirable for special purposes. For example, in the use of the plan in the selection of management trainees, there may be a case for adding to the interests and disposition sections. What should be avoided is the changing or omission of existing items, and provided this need is observed others can be put in. Even if the new ones make an attempt to break an existing item into component parts, they can reasonably be added, provided that the parent item remains.

The Seven Points

Now let us consider the seven headings, one by one, and the questions that go with them, bearing in mind the explanations and cautions already given. We shall, where it is appropriate, look not only at the interpretations which are meant to be placed on the words used, but also at the occupational relevance of the items they describe and at some main source of information about them. We may note in passing that the plan as a whole is based roughly on a series of old-fashioned dichotomies familiar to psychologists. There is a primary split between external influences (or conditions, or determinants) on which an individual's occupational success may depend, and influences that can be regarded as internal, as personal, as belonging to him, as part of his equipment. The former are here called his circumstances, the latter his attributes. His attributes (or characteristics, or qualities) are split into the mainly physical and the mainly psychological; the psychological into the mainly cognitive and the mainly non-cognitive; and these two into the natural and the acquired. We must, of course, recognise that schematisation of this sort has many limitations, and that both practical and theoretical objections can be raised to it; it has, however, the inestimable scientific advantage of encouraging observance of the principle of parsimony, and for that reason we need not hesitate to adopt it.

1: PHYSICAL MAKE-UP

Has he any defects of health or physique that may be of occupational importance?
The sooner this question is dealt with the better, because the answer to it may make further consideration of a person's suitability for a particular vacancy, or type of work, a waste of time. But there are three points to be noted. First, satisfactory conclusions about the occupational implication of a poor health record, or of a physical defect or disability, cannot usually be reached without medical aid of a

properly informed kind. Secondly, the difficulties experienced in occupational life by people handicapped in health or physique are frequently far less serious than is commonly imagined, even by doctors and potential employers. It is indeed surprising what a man with one hand or arm or leg can do with suitable tools and training and a determination not to be defeated. Thirdly, it must be realised that many of the occupational restrictions imposed on people with defects of health or physique arise, not so much from the impossibility of their meeting the demands of the work contemplated for them, as from the unwillingness of employers to take on workers who might be doubtful superannuation 'risks', or who might prove unacceptable to those with whom they would have to work.

How agreeable are his appearance, his bearing and his speech? These quasi-physical attributes are more conveniently housed under this heading than anywhere else. Their importance is generally greatest in occupations that involve frequent direct contact with people – for example, customers or clients – on whose favourable attitude the future of the enterprise largely depends. It is intended that attention should be given primarily to what may be regarded as the more enduring aspects of the trio. That is, for example, a remediable carelessness or eccentricity of dress is to be given less weight, in the assessment of appearance, than markedly unprepossessing physique or lack of 'good looks'. In the assessment of bearing, consideration is to be given to smartness and vigour rather than to such characteristics as friendliness, which belong to the section on disposition. In the assessment of speech, attention should be devoted to its physical quality, not to its fluency, which belongs to the section on special aptitudes. The separation of judgements of these three attributes is sometimes best achieved through questions of the kind: What would I think of his occupational worth, if all the knowledge I had of him had been gained from a glance at a photograph, or from passing him in the street, or from hearing him on the telephone?

Here we may note that the assessment of these and other characteristics raises the question: What are we to take as 'the average' for appearance, for bearing, for speech, and the rest? In personnel selection, it is sometimes convenient to take the average for applicants who present themselves for consideration. In vocational guidance, however, the most suitable average is often the average for people of that age, sex and type of education. Thus, on a five-step rating scale used to record judgements of the appearance of girls leaving secondary grammar schools at the age of sixteen, A might conveniently represent membership of the top ten per cent; B, of the next twenty per cent; C, of the middle forty per cent; D, of the next twenty per cent; and E, of the bottom ten per cent of that particular group.

On this basis, when we say that X is of average appearance, we mean that we would place him somewhere in the middle forty per cent of the group with which we are comparing him. An A assessment would mean that we would put him in the top ten per cent; a B assessment that we consider him to belong to the sub-group that comprise the next twenty per cent. Let us note that there is nothing right or wrong about such definitions of standards: it is a matter of convention. It is nevertheless important, for sound assessments on scales of this sort demand close adherence to whatever conventions are agreed upon. Let us note also that such rating scales are not to be regarded as 'tests' that produce judgements for us; they are merely devices for recording judgements.

2: ATTAINMENTS

What type of education has he had? How well has he done educationally? Did he finish his schooling at a secondary grammar, secondary technical or secondary modern school, or somewhere else? What evidence is there of the general standard of his scholastic achievements, compared with the average we have agreed to adopt? If he has taken the General Certificate of Education, or a School or Higher School Certificate, what indication do the results give of the general and specific nature and quality of his attainments, account being taken of the age at which he obtained them, and of any examination failures? What appear to be the school subjects in which he was stronger than other people, weaker than other people? Whether his actual levels were high or low, compared with those of others, what were his best and worst subjects? Did he win any scholarships or prizes? Did he display any occupationally ominous weaknesses in for example, English, mathematics or science? If he has had any further education, at a university or elsewhere, what has been its nature, and how well has he done in it?

These are some of the most useful questions a selector or adviser can ask himself about an applicant's educational attainments. Obviously, where he can conveniently do so, it is desirable for him to seek his evidence in part from other people – especially teachers or parents – who should be able to provide it. There are, however, two things to be noted. First, the amount of detail required will vary according to the nature of the work or training under consideration, and according to the keenness of the competition for it. Secondly, under this same heading should be gathered information about anything else the applicant has accomplished during the period of his ordinary schooling, and indeed later, provided it does not overlap wastefully with information collected in answer to the next question on the list. His membership of teams, clubs, societies, pre-Service organisations and the like should be considered; and his positions of authority and responsibility in them – and in the school itself, as a prefect, maybe – should be taken into account. So should his achievements of other kinds, whether or not they have involved membership of a group, and whether or not they have been directly concerned with his school life. In short, this question about his attainments should not be interpreted in a narrow classroom sense. It should yield all sorts of information about what he has learned and accomplished already outside the occupational field.

What occupational training and experience has he had already? How well has he done occupationally? It is important to deal here with all kinds of occupational training, from high-grade to low-grade, from theoretical to practical, from full-time to part-time, from residential to postal; and with all kinds of occupational experience. The assessor should constantly have in mind the question, What clues can I find in this individual's occupational record that will help me to make a really satisfactory prediction of his suitability for the work I have in mind for him? What does he know? What does he not know that he should know by now? What has he done? What has he not done that he should have done by now? Clearly, if the assessor is to aim at answering questions like these, he cannot be content with surface enquiries about the names of the various jobs his applicant has had, how much pay he received in them, how long he had them, and why he left. These are not unimportant, but they provide a starting-place only.

Three other points should be noted. First, although reports and testimonials sometimes have their uses in the assessment of occupational training and experience, they so often err on the side of sketchiness, leniency and equivocation that they cannot usually be regarded as of great help. However, their deficiencies can frequently be made good to an appreciable extent by the applicant himself, through careful questioning of the kind advocated above: that is, through well-conducted enquiry into what exactly he had to do in his various jobs, how he heard about them, how he was selected and trained for them (and by whom), what he found hard about them, what he disliked about them, what complaints he and his employers made about each other, to whom he was responsible, who took over his work when he was away, what kind of promotion or transfer had come to the people he replaced or worked with, and so on.

Secondly, in the course of such an enquiry much evidence can be accumulated on matters arising under most of the other headings of the Seven Point Plan. Indeed, there is often a good deal to be said for anchoring the whole assessment procedure to the investigation of attainments, to the study of knowledge already gained and skills already acquired, educationally, occupationally and in other ways; and to aim at gathering incidentally the needed information on the other points. Thirdly, it is evident that an assessor's competence in handling his exploration of his applicant's attainments will depend to a great extent on his own knowledge of the educational and occupational fields, and of common leisure activities. He cannot hope to acquire this without well-directed effort along a variety of paths.

3: GENERAL INTELLIGENCE

How much general intelligence can he display? Many faulty forecasts by selectors and advisers are traceable to failure to distinguish between a person's attainments, which show his knowledge and skill, and his general intelligence, which is his fundamental general intellectual capacity.[4, 11] It is true that the distinction is easier to make in theory than in practice, and that it is difficult to assess an individual's general intelligence except by seeing what he does with it; but this does not mean that we are reduced to judging it merely by a survey of his attainments, though this is what is often done. Rather, we must estimate it by what he manages to do with it when it is fully stretched.

The object of a general intelligence test – whether it is a group test or an individual test, whether it is verbal or non-verbal – is to provide suitable conditions for obtaining such an estimate. Carefully devised problems are presented in a carefully devised way, and the applicant's competence in tackling them is compared with the competence displayed by others in the same tasks presented in a similar way. The value of such tests for many selection and guidance purposes is now beyond dispute, except among the ignorant. There is, therefore, justification for their use in the occupational field, provided they are employed by people who are appropriately informed about the principles involved and the procedures entailed.

There are, of course, other ways of assessing a person's general intelligence –

for example, by keeping an eye open for the peaks in the record of his educational achievements, not least in mathematics and classics – but they are on the whole inferior. Nobody with sense would claim infallibility for general intelligence test results, but a good test used properly is likely to produce far fewer and far less serious mistakes than any other method of assessing fundamental general intellectual capacity. A 'good' test of general intelligence is, from the standpoint of the personnel selector and vocational adviser, one that gives a better prediction of maximum learning performance, over a wide range of activity and over a long period of time, than some other assessment procedure that might have to be used in its place.

How much general intelligence does he ordinarily display? In everyday life we recognise the fact that some people do not often use their general intelligence to the best advantage. We say, So-and-so has a good head, but he doesn't use it; or, conversely, He's not very bright, but he makes admirable use of what brains he's got. The distinction indicated by such remarks is sound and important: we must differentiate between the ceiling of a person's general intelligence and the level at which he commonly employs it, for he may tend to use it either effectively or ineffectively.

Unfortunately, tests of general intelligence do not help us here, unless they are badly given and show what a person has done in them in poorly regulated conditions rather than what he is capable of doing in conditions specially contrived to stretch him to the full.[14] We must instead depend mainly on interview estimates based in a careful study of discrepancies between his attainments, his results in general intelligence tests properly given, and the nature, range and depth of his interests; and on our appreciation of the maturity of his judgements, the realism of his aims, the precision with which he makes light on main issues in a discussion and the shrewdness with which he makes generalisations. Wilson's paper[24] offers useful comments on this problem.

4: SPECIAL APTITUDES

Has he any marked mechanical aptitude, manual dexterity, facility in the use of words or figures, talent for drawing or music? When we say that a person has a high degree of mechanical aptitude, or mechanical 'sense', we do not mean simply that he is better than most people at understanding mechanical things. He may be superior in this respect to many others, not because he has more mechanical aptitude, but because he has more general intelligence, or because he has had more opportunities for becoming interested in mechanical problems and learning how to tackle them. In fact, 'special aptitude', as we use the term here, does not mean 'unusual competence', which should be assessed under the attainments heading of the plan: it means rather, 'specialised capacity'. It is, indeed, convenient to regard all special aptitudes as talents supplementary to general intelligence in certain restricted fields: they are available to 'help' the general capacity when material of a particular kind – mechanical, manual, words, figures, drawings, music – is being handled. They are rather like auxiliary engines, whose usefulness really depends on the extent to which the main engine is powerful and effective. Where the main engine is good, the scope for the use of auxiliaries is poor.

This auxiliary role of special aptitudes is not widely appreciated. In consequence, they tend to be given more prominence than they deserve. Broadly, we are entitled to say that their occupational value is greatest in a person whose other assets are low; and their occupational importance on the whole is not comparable with the importance of general intelligence. We can rarely, if ever, claim that a certain special aptitude is 'needed' in an occupation. All we can say, usually, is that *if*, in that occupation, special competence is required in understanding mechanical things, in manipulative operations, in using words, in handling figures, in drawing or in music, *then* the possession of relevant special aptitudes will help to make up deficiencies of other kinds especially in general intelligence.

It should be noted that mechanical aptitude is most satisfactorily regarded as a specialised capacity which helps in the solution of practical-constructional problems, whether or not they are manifestly 'mechanical' in nature. Manual dexterity is a separate capacity, or cluster of capacities, which is displayed in smooth and well-timed manipulation. Facility with words may find expression in either speech or writing. Facility with figures is displayed in straightforward figure-work rather than in advanced mathematics, success in which is more closely related to general intelligence. Talent for drawing is shown in freehand rather than in machine drawing. Musical talent may be evident in critical appreciation as much as in executive performance.

Tests for special aptitudes abound. The most useful are for mechanical aptitude, and for facilities with words and figures; but even these are on the whole of far less value, in guidance and selection, than tests of general intelligence coupled with satisfactory assessments of attainments and interests. But whether or not he is using tests in his enquiries, the assessor should always remember that mere competence in a special field – mechanical, manual, words, figures, drawing, music, all these particularly – is not a necessary sign of the presence of a special aptitude. The competence may have other origins. Therefore, he must repeatedly ask himself the question, Is this person better at these things than most people of similar age, similar general intelligence, similar interests, similar opportunities? Only if the answer has to be, Yes, can he reasonably argue for the existence of a special aptitude.

5: INTERESTS

To what extent are his interests intellectual? practical–constructional? Physically-active? social? artistic? One of the commonest mistakes made in selection and guidance is to jump from a person's statement that he is interested in a thing to the conclusion that he will be good at it. He may be: he may not. The flaws in such an argument are several. In the first place, his declared interests may not tally with the interests shown by his actual behaviour. Secondly, even his genuine enthusiasms – say, for entry to a particular occupation – may be rooted in false or inadequate ideas. Thirdly, even interests that are both genuine and based on sound ideas may prove to be too short-lived to be of practical use. Fourthly, an interest may be compensatory, and indicative of a refusal to admit lack of competence[6]: it is as if someone were to say, People tell me I'm no good at this, but I'll show them! Anyway, even if a person is both good at a certain activity and interested in it, and *could* do it for a living, we are not bound to conclude that he *should*. He may be wise to keep it as a leisure pursuit, particularly if it does not easily fit in with other accomplishments and interests he might cultivate occupationally.

Despite these pitfalls, and many more, it is to his interests that we must look for indication of the directions in which his other attributes might best be employed. How shall we list them for systematic study? Should we take some catalogue of basic interests, of the kind often labelled 'instincts', and try to assess the strength of such allegedly inborn characteristics as assertiveness, gregariousness, and curiosity? Or should we adopt some other list of 'drives', of a seemingly more relevant kind, such as those towards security, independence, doing good, making money, being a centre of attraction, variety, and travel? The latter of these alternatives would be the preferable, but in practice neither would be satisfactory for general – as against specific – purposes, because what we need at least to start with, is a 'utility' list.

The method employed here is to classify interests according to a provisional fivefold classification of occupations intended for use with the Seven Point Plan. This groups occupations into (1) those involving mainly intellectual ('mental') processes, such as clerical work; (2) those of a mainly practical–constructional sort, such as engineering; (3) those of a mainly physically-active sort, such as farming; (4) those involving, essentially, some relationship with other people, such as salesmanship; and (5) those of a mainly artistic kind.

With this classification to guide us, our problem becomes largely one of investigating a person's interests – his preferred activities – to discover those that are likely to persist, whatever their origins may be; and of sorting them out according to their relevance to the main types of work available. It lays no restrictions on the range or depth or machinery of our enquiries, which can be suited to the circumstances in which our assessment has to be made: nor is it incompatible with the use of a supplementary list of 'drives' such as that given above.

6: DISPOSITION   = person's usual temperament or frame of mind.

How acceptable does he make himself to other people? Does he influence others? Is he steady and dependable? Is he self-reliant? Here we consider certain attributes frequently grouped under such headings as personality, termperament, and character. We have expressly avoided these words, because of the diversity and incompatibility of the interpretations often placed upon them, and their consequent tendency to make for confusion rather than clarity. The word 'disposition' covers well enough most of the characteristics we need to take into account for this purpose. We do in fact speak of a person as having, for example, a cheerful or retiring or calm or managing disposition, when we mean that he shows a persisting inclination to behave in these ways in circumstances in which many people would behave otherwise.

Bold question on previous page

The number of adjectives we might use for this purpose is, of course, very large[1]; but, as we have seen, for most selection and guidance procedures only a few can be chosen. The problem we face is, therefore, to decide on a short list of items of this kind that are relevant to the largest number of selection and guidance situations; that are sufficiently independent of one another to enable us to avoid the waste of time that would result if they turned out to be closely associated; and that are assessable with reasonable accuracy and consistency in the circumstances in which the assessments have usually to be made.

The four given here were listed at the end of an extensive study of the qualities of disposition most frequently taken into account by a group of experienced psychologists. For certain purposes – for example, the selection of management trainees – the list may need to be lengthened, or one or more of its items split into component parts; but it seems unlikely that any of them could safely be dropped from any assessment scheme that claimed to be comprehensive.

The first item of the four invites us to consider. How do other people take to him? How well does he 'fit in'? Does he make a good member of a group? The second, Do others take notice of what he says or does? Do his opinions carry weight? Is he good at getting people to do what he would like them to do? The third, Is his behaviour fairly predictable? Is he the sort of person to whom we might confidently say, He wouldn't do a thing like that, or, conversely, You never know what he'll do next? Does he go for long-range objectives in a determined way? The fourth, Can he stand on his own feet? Does he work things out for himself, or does he have to have somebody beside him to tell him what to do next? Does he have to be watched all the time?

It will be noticed that we have avoided the use of abstract nouns commonly employed in the study of disposition. Some of these – for example, sociability and leadership – are of doubtful value because of their lack of definiteness; but all of them are dangerous, because they have a way of encouraging unwarranted generalisation from slender evidence. The questions we have used are so worded as to fasten our attention on available facts. With these four in mind we shall be fairly well equipped for most of our assessment tasks.

7: CIRCUMSTANCES

What are his domestic circumstances? What do the other members of the family do for a living? Are there any special openings available for him? So far we have been considering our applicant's personal attributes. Now we must take account of his circumstances; that is, his background and his opportunities. Practical difficulties in the way of our doing this are, of course, very often great. In personnel selection, enquiries on these matters are often regarded as irrelevant, and are resented. In vocational guidance they are similarly viewed by some people. Clearly however, they are not irrelevant; for it is only by looking at a person's attributes in the light of his social and economic background, and in the light of the opportunities he has already had and is likely to have in the future, that we can hope to evaluate satisfactorily his past performance and make good forecasts about him.

The first question, on domestic circumstances, is essentially concerned with finance and mobility. What can he afford to do, if, for example, outlay on training or some other form of capital expenditure is needed; and how tied is he to a particular place? The second question, on the occupations of the rest of the family, is valuable, not only because it often provides a useful short-cut to relevant information about the economics, social and cultural background of the applicant, and therefore helps in the interpretation of data about his attainments, interests, and disposition; but also because in the guidance field, it may enable the adviser to steer clear of recommendations that might, for one reason or another, precipitate family conflicts. The third question, on special openings, is desirable in vocational guidance work, if only because very many people do in fact find employment in this way, regardless of other relevant considerations; and it would be foolish to ignore the fact.

References

1. ALLPORT, G. W. (1937). *Personality.* New York: Henry Holt.

2. BRITISH BROADCASTING CORPORATION (1968). *New Media and Methods in Industrial Training.* London: BBC Publications.

3. BURT, C. (1925). *The Young Delinquent.* London: University of London Press.

4. BURT, C. (1935). *The Subnormal Mind.* London: Oxford University Press.

5. CENTRAL YOUTH EMPLOYMENT EXECUTIVE (1968). *Youth Employment Manual.* Unpublished.

6. DAVIES, J. G. W. (1939). The place of interests in vocational adjustment. *Occupational Psychology.* **13**, 42–51.

7. FLANAGAN, J.C. (1949). Job Requirements. In *Current Trends in Industrial Psychology.* Pittsburgh: University of Pittsburgh Press.

8. FRASER, J. M. (1950). *A Handbook of Employment Interviewing.* London: Macdonald and Evans.

9. HEGINBOTHAM, H. (1951). *The Youth Employment Service.* London: Methuen.

10. HERON, A. (1954). Satisfaction and satisfactoriness: complementary aspects of occupational adjustment. *Occupational Psychology,* **28**, 140–153.

11. KNIGHT, R. (1933). *Intelligence and Intelligence Tests.* London: Methuen.

12. OLDFIELD, R.C. (1941). *The Psychology of the Interview.* London: Methuen.

13. RODGER, A. (1937). *A Borstal Experiment in Vocational Guidance.* IHRB Report No. 78. Medical Research Council, London: HMSO.

14. RODGER, A. (1939). The use of tests in vocational guidance. *Occupational Psychology,* **13**, 200–210.

15. RODGER, A. (1939). The Work of the Vocational Adviser. In *The Study of Society,* F. C. Bartlett *et al.* (eds.). London: Kegan Paul.

16. RODGER, A. (1945). On the selection of business executives. *Labour Management,* April-May.

17. RODGER, A. (1949). Symposium on the selection of pupils for different types of Secondary Schools. *Brit. Journal of Educ. Psychol.* **19**, 154–159.

18. RODGER, A. and CAVANAGH, P. (1968), Personnel Selection and Vocational Guidance. In Welford, A. T. *et al.* (eds.). *Society: Psychological Problems and Methods of Study.* London: Routledge and Kegan Paul.

19. RODGER, A. and DAVIES, J. G. W. (1960). Vocational Guidance and Training. In *Chambers's Encyclopaedia.* London: Newnes.

20. SUPER, D. (1957). *Vocational Development.* New York: Columbia University. Teachers College.

21. SWINDEN, J. B. (1949). *Careers in Local Government.* London: National Association of Local Government Officers.

22. VITELES, M. (1932). *Industrial Psychology.* New York: W. W. Norton.

23. VITELES, M. (1954). *Motivation and Morale in Industry.* London: Staples Press.

24. WILSON, N. A. B. (1945). Interviewing candidates for technical appointments or training. *Occupational Psychology,* **19**, 161–179.

The Seven Point Plan

1. PHYSICAL MAKE-UP
Has he any defects of health or physique that may be of occupational importance? How agreeable are his appearance, his bearing and his speech?

2. ATTAINMENTS
What type of education has he had? How well has he done educationally? What occupational training and experience has he had already? How well has he done occupationally?

3. GENERAL INTELLIGENCE
How much general intelligence can he display? How much general intelligence does he ordinarily display?

4. SPECIAL APTITUDES
Has he any marked mechanical aptitude? manual dexterity? facility in the use of words? or figures? talent for drawing? or music?

5. INTERESTS
To what extent are his interests intellectual? practical-constructional? physically-active? social? artistic?

6. DISPOSITION
How acceptable does he make himself to other people? Does he influence others? Is he steady and dependable? Is he self-reliant?

7. CIRCUMSTANCES
What are his domestic circumstances? What do the other members of the family do for a living? Are there any special openings available for him?

General Intelligence controls every aspect of mental ability to some degree, so that performance on *every* intelligence or aptitude test is affected to some extent by 'g', according to the theory. The two 'departmental managers' control two further broad areas of ability in such a way that every test is influenced by one or other of them. Tests which tap people's ability with words or figures are affected by verbal–educational (i.e. scholastic) ability, and tend to be useful for predicting performance in written examinations (even in technical subjects). Performance on tests of mechanical and spatial* aptitude is controlled by the second 'departmental manager'. This broad area of ability also tends to be related to performance in technical subjects, and to practical trades such as vehicle mechanics and toolsetting.

In the Seven Point Plan, Alec Rodger used a different analogy to illustrate the predominance of General Intelligence over the Special Aptitudes:

> They are rather like auxiliary engines, whose usefulness really depends on the extent to which the main engine is powerful and effective. Where the main engine is good, the scope for the use of auxiliaries if poor. (7PP,pp.9–10)

The auxiliaries are of course the Special Aptitudes: 'talents supplementary to general intelligence in certain restricted fields'. (7PP,p.9)

Fundamental to this approach is the idea that people with high 'g' will be 'good at everything' and score highly on special aptitude tests as well as general intelligence tests. The 'higher authority' of General Intelligence can overrule the Special Aptitudes. According to the Plan, a person might obtain a high score on a mechanical aptitude test either (a) because they possess high mechanical aptitude or (b) because they have high General Intelligence or even (c) because they have 'had more opportunities for becoming interested in mechanical problems and learning how to tackle them' (7PP,p.9). And presumably the high score could also be caused by some combination of these three factors.

---

* 'Spatial' is the adjective from 'space'; spatial aptitude is the ability to visualise and mentally manipulate shapes and to understand the relationship between shapes, e.g. being able to visualise the layout of a building.

It also follows from the Plan that Special Aptitudes are more important when 'g' is low. Someone having high General Intelligence doesn't need a Special Aptitude to perform well on a special aptitude test – their high *General* Intelligence will guarantee a good performance. On the other hand a person with low General Intelligence cannot do well on a special aptitude test unless they possess the aptitude which it measures (leaving aside the question of opportunity, which a well-designed test would bracket out anyway). We need to know more about the Special Aptitudes of people with relatively low 'g' because they depend more on having the necessary Special Aptitudes in order to be good at something. When the chief executive is weak, the managers play a greater role!

So runs the argument (7PP,pp,9–10), and the theory on which Alec Rodger's description of General Intelligence and Special Aptitudes is founded. He gives General Intelligence overwhelming emphasis:

> We can rarely, if ever, claim that a certain special aptitude is 'needed' in an occupation. All we can say, usually, is that if, in that occupation, special competence is required in understanding mechanical things, in manipulative operations, in using words, in handling figures, in drawing or in music, *then* the possession of relevant special aptitudes will help to make up deficiencies of other kinds especially in general intelligence.

But what *is* this mysterious, all-embracing factor? And how does it differ from the Special Aptitudes? The distinction is not made any clearer by the apparent similarity between items contained in special aptitude tests and those to be found in tests which claim to measure 'g'. At first sight there appears to be little difference between, say, the numerical questions contained in AH3* – which is supposed to measure general ability – and those in sections of the General Clerical Test, or the diagrammatic items in AH6 and the content of the DAT Abstract Reasoning Test. This confuses many people. Where does General Intelligence end and Special Aptitude begin?

---

* The tests quoted in this section are described in the NFER-NELSON Catalogue of Tests for Industry and Commerce.[18]

The existence of positive correlations* between virtually all ability tests – even apparently dissimilar ones such as verbal reasoning and mechanical comprehension – has provided support for the concept of a 'universal ability'. However, the fact that most ability tests are positively correlated does not *necessarily* mean that there is some underlying ability which affects all of them. There are other possible explanations for such intercorrelations – e.g. there could be a large number of component elements or 'logic circuits', some of which were common to all abilities which tests measure. And we tend to overlook the fact that cognitive tests do have some common features, like written instructions! The ability to understand and follow written instructions arguably affects performance on *all* tests (even computerised ones).

The author found a correlation of .67 between a verbal reasoning test and a mechanical comprehension test among a group of approximately 100 Zambian subjects, and smaller but still significant correlations between verbal and spatial/mechanical tests in the UK. These correlations could be interpreted as evidence of a general factor, but they are just as likely to be accounted for by the level of verbal comprehension required in tests such as the Bennett Mechanical Comprehension Test. Some candidates take much longer than others to assimilate the written instructions alongside each question, and to this extent it is measuring English comprehension/verbal reasoning as well as mechanical aptitude.

More recently, there has been some evidence to suggest that zero or even negative correlations between tests do occur.

---

* Correlation is a statistical technique for establishing the degree of association between two variable characteristics. For example if those candidates who obtain high scores on Test A also tend to score highly on Test B, and those who obtain low scores on Test A also tend to obtain low scores on Test B, there is a positive correlation between the two tests. Conversely, a negative correlation would exist if people who do well on Test A tend to do badly on Test B. The exact degree of association is established by calculating the correlation coefficient, which can vary between − 1.0 and + 1.0. In everyday life, height and weight are two characteristics which are positively correlated, while there is a negative correlation between daily rainfall and sunshine figures. Although the significance of a particular value of a correlation coefficient is affected by the size of the sample on which it is based, generally speaking a coefficient of .25 or more (whether positive or negative) indicates a definite association between the two 'variables'.

The controversy surrounding General Intelligence can be boiled down to the following questions:

1.   Does it exist as a separate entity?
2.   If so, what is it?
3.   How important is it, relative to other factors?

By and large, British and European psychologists have tended to attach great importance to the general factor and give less attention to special factors, while American psychologists have tended to do exactly the opposite. There is therefore a substantial difference in approach between psychologists working on opposite sides of the Atlantic, but it is a difference of emphasis rather than a total disagreement. Most theories of mental ability are based on the findings of a complex statistical procedure called factor analysis* and to a large extent the discrepancies between them can be explained by differences between the statistical techniques employed by different investigators to analyse test intercorrelations. Different statistical techniques applied to different sets of test scores would be likely to produce different results!

It is also broadly true that studies supporting the general factor have been based mainly on children, whilst those 'disconfirming' it have been based on college students. Garrett[19] proposed the idea that there is increasing differentiation of abilities with age, and there is some evidence to support this interesting suggestion. Young children have tended to obtain more uniform results, and older children have been found to have more definite strengths and weaknesses. Unfortunately, as with so much psychological research, other studies have found the opposite. In any case Garrett's theory is very difficult to prove.

The answers to the three questions posed earlier therefore seem fairly negative. The concept of General Intelligence is ill-

---

* Factor analysis is a statistical procedure for identifying the underlying ability factors which determine performance on different kinds of test. There are several methods of factor analysis, but the first step in the procedure is always the administration of a number of different kinds of test to a large sample of people. Correlation coefficients are then calculated between every possible pair of tests, and the resulting table of intercorrelations is analysed so that the factors may be established. Factors identified by means of this procedure are of course nothing more than statistical abstractions.

defined and it is doubtful whether 'g' exists or whether general intelligence tests measure anything different from special aptitude tests. The concept of General Intelligence *as a separate entity* has been so widely questioned that it is perhaps better abandoned. The 'American' view of abilities as an array of specialised abilities is theoretically sound and does not require us to assume that there is any underlying general factor. Thurstone's[20] Primary Mental Abilities and the eight subtests of the Differential Aptitude Tests (DAT)[21] are typical examples of this approach. They both show some resemblance to the six Special Aptitudes listed in the Plan:

Primary Mental Abilities	Differential Aptitude Tests	Seven Point Plan
verbal meaning	verbal reasoning ⎫	
	spelling	facility with words
verbal fluency	language usage ⎭	
numerical ability	numerical ability	facility with figures
	mechanical reasoning	mechanical aptitude
spatial ability	space relations	talent for drawing
inductive reasoning	abstract reasoning	
	clerical speed and accuracy	
perceptual speed		
		manual dexterity
		talent for music
rote memory		

It would be possible to work out a composite or average score on the eight subtests on the DAT to provide a measure of general ability, but note that this would not be the same as using a test of general intelligence. Not only have American psychologists tended to minimise the importance of General Intelligence; they have also altered its definition. Instead of treating it as a separately measurable entity they have viewed it as a composite or average of other abilities.

What about the original half dozen Special Aptitudes in the Plan? Most of them still stand up fairly well, but 'talent for drawing' would be better described as 'spatial ability'. This ability to visualise and mentally manipulate shapes has much broader applications than 'talent for drawing'. Spatial ability tests have related well to such diverse activities as technical drawing, engineering design, computing and dentistry. It might also be worth adding some composite abilities such as clerical/secretarial and computer programming to the original list. Again, our description of aptitudes is more pragmatic nowadays and less tied to one particular theory of mental ability. Few test manuals now quote the findings of factor analysis (see above) to show what a test is supposed to be measuring. Instead, test manuals tend to show correlations between the test and other tests, or with aspects of work performance which it might reasonably be expected to predict, such as marks in an examination at the end of a training course. This allows users to draw their own conclusions.

Another possible addition to the list of abilities might be the much-maligned concept of creativity. For the sake of completeness there does seem to be an argument for including 'creative' or 'open-ended' or 'divergent' reasoning, despite the fact that creativity tests have had limited success and in some cases have shown high correlations with general ability tests. Divergent reasoning is the opposite of convergent reasoning, as measured by 'conventional' ability tests. Conventional tests almost always contain problems which have one, and only one, correct solution. Creativity tests require a variety of answers, such as the classic 'How many uses can you think of for a brick?'

There are many other considerations in assessing ability, such as the importance of memory, the effects of cultural differences on test performance, and so on. Some issues are of no practical significance (to selectors), such as the relative importance of heredity and environment in determining intelligence.

The emphasis has been on testing because tests have contributed so much to our understanding of mental abilities. There are other ways of assessing intelligence and aptitudes, but, as Alec Rodger acknowledges, 'they are on the whole inferior'. (7PP,pp.8–9) An interview is particularly unreliable in this respect, because fluency is easily mistaken for intelligence. However, as in other areas, a more accurate interview assessment of intelligence and aptitudes can be made by concentrating on biographical information. Performance in science subjects, particularly mathematics, is a guide to numeracy and abstract reasoning ability. Coverage of interests may also reveal special competence in a particular area (e.g. someone with a very strong interest in microcomputing may have published programs in a personal computer journal). Like Disposition, General Intelligence and Special Aptitudes are areas of inference (see Figure 1), and are best assessed in the interview by making inferences from the areas of exploration, particularly Attainments and Interests.

The distinction which Alec Rodger makes between potential and displayed intelligence is not particularly useful. The question 'How much intelligence does he ordinarily display?' seems capable of being answered by an assessment of Attainments: 'How well has he done educationally/occupationally?' There seems to be little difference between Attainments and displayed intelligence as these two concepts are explained in the Plan.

The arguments about intelligence and ability have been discussed at some length to enable the reader to take a critical look at the Plan's description of these areas. There does seem to be a simpler and more plausible way of classifying human abilities than that given in the Plan, although the description of the Special Aptitudes themselves needs little alteration. The revised classification of abilities would run along the following lines.

ABILITIES

Human abilities can be classified at several levels. Some abilities are so specific that they are only likely to relate to one particular job or aspect of a job. Others (roughly equivalent to the Special Aptitudes in the Seven Point Plan) are broader and of more general interest. These broad aptitudes are the first main level of classification and include verbal comprehension and fluency, numerical aptitude (often referred to as numeracy), spatial aptitude, mechanical aptitude and diagrammatic or abstract reasoning. Other possible additions to the list include musical aptitude, manual dexterity (although this is not a purely mental ability), creativity, memory, and groups of abilities which span two or more of the aptitudes already mentioned. Examples of these ability groupings include clerical aptitude and the scholastic aptitude composite of the Differential Aptitude Tests. We may be interested in assessing a very specific ability, or in one or more of the broader aptitudes, depending on the job for which we are selecting.

There are two very broad clusters or groupings of ability at the next level: scholastic and technical. Most aptitudes tend to fall into one or other of these two areas. **Scholastic** ability comprises verbal comprehension and numerical aptitude, but verbal fluency and perhaps musical ability are also associated with this category. (Musical aptitude seems to be the most separate of all the aptitudes.) **Technical** ability comprises spatial and mechanical aptitude, abstract reasoning and perhaps manual dexterity. In careers work knowledge of a person's performance over both areas can greatly assist in deciding whether a person's abilities are better suited to non-technical arts/commercial or scientific/technical careers, respectively. Most people have a relative strength in one or other area. Some people obtain similar scores on both verbal/numerical and spatial/mechanical/abstract tests, and a small minority obtain very high scores on all of them. In the old days we would have said that these people had high General Intelligence.

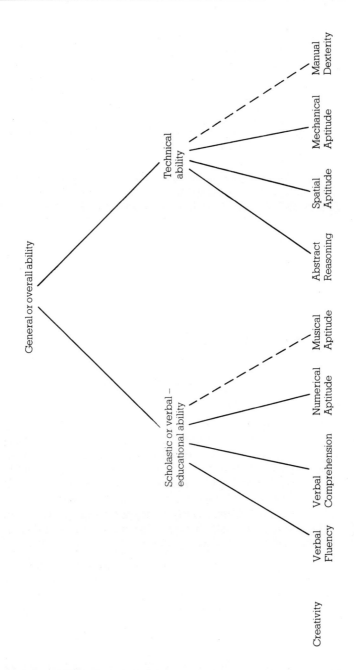

Figure 5: THE MAIN AREAS OF HUMAN ABILITY
(Each level is a subdivision of the one above it)

Interests

As with abilities, the most economical and useful way of describing Interests seems to be in terms of a few broad groupings, using more detailed descriptions as the need arises. Thus a job may require (or it may be highly desirable to possess) an interest in people in general (e.g. sales representative, travel courier). As long as a candidate shows some evidence of interest in entertaining/helping/persuading/understanding or just being with other people this may be sufficient. On other occasions it may be necessary to specify the required interest in more detail. Someone may need to have an interest in helping people in a relatively superficial way (e.g. running an information desk) or by forming relatively long-term relationships with them (e.g. teaching). These two activities are obviously different, and a candidate may produce evidence appropriate to one rather than the other. Equally a person whose social interests only take the form of entertaining people of a similar social level might not be suited to either.

Like abilities and personality, therefore, Interests can be classified in terms of a few broad categories or many narrow ones. Specific interests are rarely if ever an essential requirement on a personnel specification, but broad areas of interest certainly could be. We would probably never require a candidate to be interested in football or even electronics, although these interests might be highly desirable for certain kinds of work. But evidence of outdoor or intellectual interests *of some kind* could well be a requirement.

The economy of the Seven Point Plan's classification of Interests is therefore an attractive feature. Most interest inventories have upwards of six categories (e.g. the Vocational Preference Inventory[18] and Rothwell-Miller Interest Blank[18] have eleven and twelve respectively). A small number of more or less independent categories has a distinct appeal. T.E. Lawrence in *Seven Pillars of Wisdom* suggested only three – people, things and ideas – and this is hard to beat as a simple way of classifying a person's priorities.

Having said this, one or two of the Plan's Interest categories seem rather unsatisfactory. And, like the dispositional categories, they are not directly related to any test. Alec Rodger subsequently proposed the term 'scientific–technical' in place of 'practical–constructional', but this alteration does not seem very helpful. In fact it might be argued that these are distinct and useful categories of Interest which should *both* be included, with practical–constructional being the more practical and scientific–technical the more intellectual ends of the same continuum.

The use of the word 'artistic' seems to suggest a rather narrow and irrelevant area. The term 'aesthetic' might be an improvement, to include interest in, sensitivity to and enjoyment of one's surroundings. Interests in art, architecture, landscape, photography, home decorating, philately etc could all fall within this broad 'aesthetic' category. It would perhaps be more relevant to industrial selection than 'artistic interest', e.g. by encouraging us to consider how susceptible a person might be to noise and visual pollution.

The fivefold classification of Interests in the Seven Point Plan is nevertheless a practical and useful device for making sense of a person's specific interests and activities. The fact that someone is interested in amateur dramatics, for instance, is not likely to be very significant in itself. It could be positively misleading if we simply assume that the person concerned is interested in people, or the arts. An interest in amateur dramatics could indicate real interest in any one of the five categories, or a combination of them. The Plan categories help us to look at the satisfactions people derive from their interests and activities, rather than at the activities themselves, and to try to match the satisfactions which the job can offer with the candidate's *areas* of interest.

Alec Rodger also emphasised the important distinction between Interests and abilities. To his comments about assuming that a person is good at something because they are interested in it, one might add the observation that a mismatch between interests and abilities can cause serious problems in career choice. A person whose interests and abilities diverge faces a difficult prospect: mediocrity in a career chosen on the basis of interest, or dissatisfaction in one chosen on grounds of ability. A compromise is not always feasible, even assuming that the individual has the self-awareness to understand the problem. Many people with strong verbal/scholastic abilities are keenly interested in science and technology. A career in technical journalism is not necessarily a very satisfactory compromise for them. Conversely, people channelled into a career in science or engineering because their best subjects at school were mathematics and science occasionally throw it all up for social work or hotel management, where they can satisfy their main interest (in people) rather than use their main ability (in science).

Although Interests is an important area of assessment in its own right, it is equally important – as a means to an end – in assessing Disposition. Much can be learnt about the sixth point from a thorough coverage of the fifth. If we discover that a candidate who says he is very keen on amateur dramatics is mainly involved in sound or lighting, this suggests that his interest is primarily an intellectual/technical one. If he only gets involved in 'backstage' activities, this again suggests that social and artistic interests might be of secondary importance. His Interest priorities in turn can reveal much about acceptability, influence, self-reliance and dependability. A person's reasons for pursuing a particular interest can also be highly significant.

There is a strong case for incorporating **motivation** into the Plan, but it is at first difficult to see how this can be done. Apart from the fact that there seem to be as many definitions of motivation as there are of intelligence, motivation does seem to be intrinsically different from the existing points in the sense that it is partly situational. Unlike the seven points, it is unstable, and partly determined by the situation in which a person finds themself. Even health and present circumstances are relatively stable in comparison to motivation, although of course they too can change very suddenly! General Intelligence, Special Aptitudes and Disposition are stable within fairly narrow limits and the pattern of a person's Interests also tends to be consistent (although the interests themselves may alter). Past attainments and early background are completely unalterable.

One solution would be to add **self-motivation** to the Plan, or even achievement motivation, and try to estimate how far a person's self-motivation would be likely to fit in with what a job can or cannot offer. This concept would include such frequently-quoted terms as drive, ambition, vigour etc. The trouble is that self-motivation is also a difficult concept to define, and anything which is difficult to define is going to be difficult to assess.

Another problem is that motivation tends to be given a different emphasis in careers guidance and personnel selection. In vocational guidance work the concern is mainly with a person's intrinsic self-motivation and longer term aims (what drives them and in which directions?) This aspect of motivation is arguably a fairly stable attribute which fits in well with the original points in the Plan. In selection, however, we also need to assess the candidate's motivation towards a particular vacancy (what are their reasons for applying for this particular job?) This aspect of motivation is ephemeral, influenced as it is by the particular combination of factors – dissatisfaction in present job, need for security or change, relative pay and conditions, etc – operating at a particular point in time. Yet there is a need to include this **ad hoc motivation** in our classification system, regardless of its instability.

It is useful to assess ad hoc motivation in terms of positive and negative reasons. Does the candidate give mainly positive reasons for applying, or mainly negative ones? It is not too difficult to distinguish between them, as the following examples (taken from application forms and interview statements) illustrate:

Positive reasons	**Negative reasons**
To move into —	To move out of —
To enter a new field of employment	Redundancy in previous post
To gain experience	Dissatisfaction
Greater responsibility, challenge etc.	Total disillusionment in previous post
Better salary, conditions etc.	Personality clashes in previous post
Career progression	No prospects

The omission of motivation from the Seven Point Plan has caused much confusion and has led many interviewers to avoid making judgements about this important area. Another reason for stressing motivation is that it seems to be one of the areas which interviewers can assess more accurately. It has been included in this revision by popular demand, using a simple classification scheme.

MOTIVATION

The word motivation seems to be used to describe (at least) three separate constructs. The first is the Interest area already contained in the original Plan; the other two are additional to it. The list of **Interests** provides a simple system for classing the **type** of interest(s) which a person has. **Self-motivation** describes the

strength or **level** of motivation generally. **Aims** describes the
direction of motivation.

Type	**Level**
Interests/priorities	*Self-motivation*
Intellectual	Vigour/drive/energy
Practical–constructional	Strength of achievement need
Physically active/outdoor	
Social	
Aesthetic	

Direction
Aims
Ad hoc motivation: positive/negative reasons
Longer term career aims

Disposition = person's usual temperament or frame of mind.

In some ways Disposition is the least satisfactory of all the seven points. Alec Rodger's reservations about the use of the word 'personality' seem rather strange, since 'Disposition' seems just as confusing and even more obscure. 'Personality' is almost universally accepted in psychological and 'lay' circles and is surely not a particularly emotive or difficult term nowadays. Most personality questionnaires or tests are:

a) *called* personality questionnaires; and
b) measure personality characteristics which are difficult to reconcile with the four aspects of Disposition listed in the Plan.

Four attributes of Disposition – acceptability, influence, self-reliance and dependability – emerged from an informal study carried out by the staff of the National Institute of Industrial Psychology many years ago, and were subsequently found to be similar to a list drawn up by an Army research team. (However, this hardly provides evidence of their validity as psychological concepts. Psychologists might call it 'coincidental validity'!)

'Acceptability', 'influence', 'self-reliance' and 'dependability' are useful descriptions of personality areas, but plentiful evidence about 'real' personality characteristics is now available from numerous personality tests and it would be a pity to ignore it in any revision of the Plan. It seems curious that the Plan's description of personality was drawn up in such an 'unscientific' way when General Intelligence and Special Aptitudes were so closely linked to the psychological theories of the time.

Although some intuitive connections can be made between the four dispositional characteristics and some of the characteristics measured by personality questionnaires, the former seem simplistic and rather inadequate, even for selection purposes. They were not derived from tests, nor have any tests ever been devised to assess them. It is also slightly confusing that 'acceptability' and 'influence' seem to be descriptions of how a person is seen by others (e.g. How do other people take to him? Do others take notice of what he says or does?) whereas 'dependability' and 'self-reliance' sound more like 'internal' personality traits. Acceptability and influence are also liable to be confused with aspects of Physical Make-up such as appearance, bearing and speech.

Figure 6 is an attempt to relate a number of test-based personality characteristics to each other and to the four Dispositions. Despite differences in theoretical background and approach there are similarities between many of these characteristics. This kind of analysis should be a starting-point for a more satisfactory Seven Point Plan description of personality, which should also include attributes that have most commonly been shown to be valid in selection (e.g. sociability and ascendancy on the Gordon Personal Profile have been found to be related to managerial success).

Some of the differences between the tests themselves can be attributed to deliberate differences in approach by test authors. For example, the FIRO[18] tests set out to measure interpersonal aspects, while the Edwards Personal Preference Schedule[18] is based on a particular theory of needs and motives.

Other interesting personality descriptions have been suggested. One example is the 'Type A' personality/behaviour pattern which has been associated with coronary heart disease and even business success (Boyd, 1984).[22] Type A individuals are 'aggressively involved in a chronic, incessant struggle to achieve more and more in less and less time', Type B individuals are supposed to be 'relaxed, patient and altogether more passive.' (Jenkins, 1979)[23]

Some research workers also claim to have found evidence of overlap between vocational interests and personality. One analysis of responses to interest questionnaires and personality inventories produced six underlying dimensions of interest-and-personality.[24] Holland[25] says that 'interest inventories are essentially personality inventories' and his Vocational Preference Inventory contains eleven scales (e.g. realistic, social, self-control) which sound like personality dimensions.

There therefore seems to be less agreement about personality characteristics than about any other areas of assessment. As with abilities and Interests, there are trade-offs between the broadness or specificity of factor descriptions, and their degree of separateness or relatedness. The Seven Point Plan proposed four broad, conceptually separate characteristics but they lack detail (and seem out of step with other personality descriptions). The 16PF[18] provides us with a larger number of more specific factors, but they do not correspond very closely with everyday descriptions of personality and are often quite closely related to each

16PF (more specific factors in bracket)	Eysenck Personality Inventory (EPI)	Edwards Personal Preference Schedule (EPPS)	Gordon Personal Profile (GPP)	FIRO	Myers–Briggs Type Indicator (MBTI)	Seven Point Plan
introversion–extraversion (reserved–outgoing; sober–happy-go-lucky; shy–venturesome, socially bold)	introversion–extraversion	exhibition$_2$	sociability$_{1,2,3}$	inclusion$_3$	introversion–extraversion	acceptability
subduedness–independence (humble–assertive)		deference, dominance	ascendancy$_{1,2,4}$	openness, control$_4$		influence
adjustment–anxiety (emotionally stable–affected by feelings; self-assured–apprehensive, relaxed–tense)	stability–neuroticism		emotional stability			
tough poise–emotionality		nurturance$_5$, affiliation$_6$, order$_7$, autonomy$_8$			thinking–feeling$_{5,6}$, sensing$_7$–intuition$_8$, judging, perceiving$_8$	self-reliance?
(undisciplined self-conflict–controlled, socially precise; expedient–conscientious)			responsibility			dependability?

FIGURE 6: WORDS USED TO DESCRIBE PERSONALITY CHARACTERISTICS IN SIX PERSONALITY TESTS AND IN THE SEVEN POINT PLAN. (Terms which seem closest in meaning are shown in the same row). N.B. Correlations have been found between those having the same numbered subscripts.

other. In the author's view the Gordon Personal Profile and Inventory provides a good compromise between detail and economy.[18] The Gordon scales measure eight reasonably independent personality characteristics (six of which were originally derived from the 16PF). They are:

Ascendancy	Cautiousness
Responsibility	Original thinking
Emotional stability	Personal relations
Sociability	Vigour

The new Occupational Personality Questionnaires[26] offer a number of scales designed to assess aspects of relating to people, thinking style and feeling. Within these three broad areas it is possible to assess five major dimensions (e.g. emotionally stable, vigorous) or up to 30 more specific ones (e.g. relaxed, optimistic, decisive).

One is therefore faced with a dilemma in updating the Seven Point Plan's description of dispositional characteristics. On the one hand there is a need to expand the Plan's descriptions and bring them into line with current theory. On the other hand there is a danger of producing yet another permutation of words.

The suggested classification of personality characteristics shown at the end of this section is derived from a number of sources, including Figure 6. The main headings are an attempted summary of points of agreement in test research. The sub-headings are component descriptions which may be useful when more detail is needed.

Thinking style is included in this system because it seems to be an important and perhaps rather neglected personality dimension. Few would disagree that there seem to be marked differences in people's habitual or preferred styles of thinking, and that these differences help to determine suitability for different kinds of work and may cause problems in interpersonal relationships.

The Myers-Briggs Type Indicator (MBTI)[18] presents a classification of this area of personality in terms of perception and judgement. Perception is defined as the process of becoming aware (of things, people, or events). Judgement is the process of reaching conclusions about what has been perceived. According to Isabel Briggs Myers,[27] people tend to prefer either perceiving or judging as a habitual way of dealing with 'the outside world'.

'Perceivers' and 'judgers' in turn can each be divided into two further categories. Some people who prefer perceiving to judging rely mainly on factual details (sensing), whilst others are intuitive and tend to add their own ideas or associations. Those who prefer judging to perceiving can be divided into those who prefer to judge impersonally on the basis of true or false (thinking), and those who make more personal judgements according to whether or not they value something (feeling). Finally, extraverts prefer to focus their perceptions or judgements on people and things, whilst introverts look inwards to concepts and ideas. Myers's descriptions of these various 'types' ring true, and show some relationship to other personality dimensions (see Figure 6). Her test is used to identify similar or contrasting types for team-building purposes, and also for counselling and selection.

The Kirton Adaption–Innovation Inventory (KAI)[28] measures two creative thinking styles. Adaptors prefer to initiate changes which improve procedures within established frames of reference, while innovators are likely to generate more radical solutions and challenge the way in which a problem has previously been defined. Kirton has found correlations between innovation and the Myers-Briggs factors of perception and intuition.[29] (The Kirton Inventory is a test of creative style, not creative ability.)

Although personality questionnaires and inventories have helped to build up a body of knowledge, none of them provide a complete description of personality characteristics, nor are they the only source of information about personality. At best, personality questionnaires provide some valuable insights, usually from a particular theoretical standpoint. Some, like the 16PF or OPQ, present a comprehensive listing of personality traits, but trait theory is not the only approach to personality assessment. Personality is too complex to be adequately described in terms of lists of attributes, even if they have been established by mathematically impeccable procedures. They sound rather like the 'mere bundle of "qualities" ' against which Alec Rodger warned us.

There is, for example, the question of 'mood', 'state' and flexibility. In effect, a trait score on a personality inventory merely represents the person's 'average' position for that particular characteristic. It is the point of equilibrium to which a person returns when situational demands are not pushing them in one or other direction. Everyone's displayed personality shows some variability, and some people probably vary their behaviour more than others.

Flexibility of behaviour is surely an important personality dimension in itself. One person will show little variation in terms of, say, extraversion, while another person with exactly the same extraversion score on a personality test will behave quite differently in different situations. If the situation calls for it – or perhaps if the mood takes them – the latter individual will be more introverted and reflective, or on the other hand even more outgoing and extraverted, than the basic score would suggest. Reddin[30] proposed the term 'style flex' to describe flexibility of management style in his '3-D' theory of managerial effectiveness. We could use the same term to describe flexibility of personality in general. It could also be dubbed 'the chameleon factor'. Flexibility in this sense is not the same thing as adaptability. The term 'adaptability' tends to be used to describe a person's ability to adapt permanently to permanently changed situations.

Reversal theory (Smith and Apter, 1975; Apter, 1982)[31,32] is an interesting attempt to describe aspects of personality in terms of dominant states rather than traits. By so doing, it contributes to our understanding of personality **dynamics.** (Actually reversal theory is described as a theory of motivation.)

The theory puts forward the idea that there are two opposite motivational states or modes, and that people switch from one to the other (hence reversal). In the 'telic' state, high arousal is experienced as unpleasant and anxiety-producing, and the individual aims for 'a quiet life'. People in the telic mode experience lack of stimulation as pleasant relaxation. In the opposite, 'paratelic', state, high arousal is experienced as pleasant excitement, while low arousal is experienced as boredom.

Murgatroyd et al. (1978)[33] use the term 'dominance' to indicate a person's usual or preferred mode of behaviour, but even a person with a strong preference for the paratelic mode will reverse and exhibit telic behaviour on occasions, just as a telic-dominant person will sometimes 'freak out' and behave paratelically. Reversal theorists are interested in the factors which cause these reversals to occur (or not occur), and have attempted to relate their theory to a wide range of physical and psychological variables. Reversals into the paratelic state may be a reason for 'mindless violence' and other apparently irrational acts.

There seems to be little overlap between telic/paratelic dominance and other personality dimensions such as introversion or the 16PF factors. Although a preference for telic behaviour shows some association with introversion, they are by no means the same thing. This suggests that the concept of telic/paratelic dominance is a useful addition to our catalogue of personality descriptions. Telic dominance is also distinct from the Type A behaviour described above – it is possible to be a Type A (restless, achievement-motivated) telic dominant person, or a Type B (relaxed, passive) paratelic. Reversal theory and Myers's type theory have something in common: they both attempt to explain aspects of personality in terms of compensatory mental processes or **modes.** 'Mode' theories assume that a person may behave differently in different situations and on different occasions.

Myers's type theory holds that each individual has a preferred or *dominant* mental process – either sensing or intuition, thinking or feeling – but that their less preferred *auxiliary* process provides an important counterbalance. The strength of the dominant process and the degree of development of the auxiliary is a matter of prime concern in any assessment based on the Type Indicator:

> If a person has no obvious development of an auxiliary process, the absence is likely to be obvious. An extreme perceptive with no judgement is all sail and no rudder. An extreme judging type with no perception is all form and no content.[27]

Similarly in reversal theory the focus of interest is on the strength of telic or paratelic dominance and the conditions under which the person is likely to reverse into the alternative state.

'Mode' theories provide an interesting corollary to the trait theory which underlies most personality tests. Neither approach provides a complete account of personality, but both help to increase our overall understanding of personality dynamics.

PERSONALITY

Main dimensions are underlined, with component traits shown underneath. Each trait description should be taken to include its opposite (e.g. someone who was the opposite of dominant would be described as submissive). In the case of thinking style both ends of the scale of measurement are given, because the word used to describe the opposite end of the scale is not always opposite in meaning (e.g. Judging-Perceiving).

Outgoing/extraverted (16PF, EPI, MBTI)

Gregarious	*Assertive*
Inclusion (FIRO)	Assertive (16PF)
Sociability (GPP)	Dominant (EPPS)
Exhibition (EPPS)	Ascendancy (GPP)
Acceptable (7PP)	Control (FIRO)
Openness (FIRO)	Influence (7PP)

Calm and emotionally stable

Emotionally Stable (16PF); Emotional stability (GPP)
Self-confident/self-assured (16PF)
Relaxed (16PF)
Stability (EPI)

Independent and self-reliant

Autonomy (EPPS)
Self-reliant (7PP)

Conscientious and dependable

Responsibility (GPP)
Controlled, socially precise (16PF)
Conscientious (16PF)
Steady and dependable (7PP)

Thinking style

	–	Original Thinking (GPP)
Closed	–	Open
Convergent	–	Divergent
Judging	–	Perceiving
(Thinking–Feeling)	–	(Sensing–Intuition)
Adaptor	–	Innovator

Personality dynamics

What are the results of the person's unique combination of traits?
How much 'style flex' do they display?
How much variation in motivational state?
How do they react to situational demands?

Circumstances

If Physical Make-up is the most overrated area of the Seven Point Plan, Circumstances is surely the most underrated. Many interviewers pay scant attention to candidates' family background or current circumstances. Perhaps they feel that the former is irrelevant and the latter an invasion of privacy. More experienced selectors, who have learned the hard way, acknowledge the contribution of these two areas to the selection equation.

> ...it is only by looking at a person's attributes in the light of his social and economic background, and in the light of the opportunities he has already had and is likely to have in the future, that we can hope to evaluate satisfactorily his past performance and make good forecasts about him. (7PP,p.12)

Actually, Alec Rodger did not make a clear distinction between early background and present circumstances (in the case of young people, they do tend to merge). His three sub-headings – 'Domestic circumstances', 'Family occupations' and 'Special openings' – seem to refer primarily to *present* circumstances.

However, an assessment of the person's achievements is surely incomplete – not to say unfair – unless it is set against the background of their opportunities. As with school education, there are many examples where an understanding of early background alters one's overall assessment of the person.

Chronic sickness in early childhood may have caused prolonged absences from school, which in turn may be seen as a possible reason for poor social skills or negative attitudes towards education that have persisted into adulthood. In one case a severe injury kept an individual away from school until the age of twelve. Understandably, he found it very difficult to adjust to classroom education, having been educated by a private tutor until that time. He experienced rejection by other children, and developed a strong antipathy towards school which he still felt. His academic record after leaving school has, however, been impressive, and he has pursued a successful career in marketing.

Although early background rarely has such a marked effect, the checklist principle demands that it should be included in our data collection procedure. Every now and then, our brief check will reveal something significant to the overall assessment. For instance, if two candidates have identical educational qualifications, but one has obtained them in the face of great obstacles, this is surely useful additional data. Once again, we can see the interconnectedness of the different points – in this case, an examination of Circumstances has produced evidence of dispositional qualities (self-reliance, determination, dependability). Family background is particularly important in assessing young people. We surely do them an injustice by not taking account of the possible effects of domestic upheavals or parental disapproval of their activities. Early background tends to assume greatest importance in a careers guidance interview with a young person because of the influence of parental attitudes and other factors (such as family income) on occupational choice.

Of course, early background should be kept in perspective. Given the very limited time available, it is not worth more than a brief mention in most selection interviews.

If the case for covering early background is somewhat difficult to defend, that for present circumstances certainly is not. It is strange that some interviewers with strong views about their 'right to know' in other areas, shy away from asking questions about domestic, financial or other commitments which might easily determine whether somebody is successful in a job. In the author's experience, Circumstances are discussed in a minority of selection interviews, and early background is rarely mentioned. Candidates are probably much more willing to answer questions about personal circumstances than interviewers are to ask them. The barrier to communication seems to be on the interviewer's side of the table, not the interviewee's.

Present circumstances is concerned with outside factors which could affect availability to work, or performance at work. The following questions are relevant:

How far does the person have to travel to work? (But how often/how quickly do they need to be there?)

Able to travel as the job requires within UK/abroad/live abroad?

Able to drive?

Able/willing to relocate/partner's attitude towards relocation/effects of relocation on children's education, etc?

Dependent relatives?

Financial commitments?

Religious, social, political, and other commitments?

Any special openings?

N.B. As with all the preceding points, this is only being put forward as a checklist. In many cases some of these items will be irrelevant, i.e. they will not appear on the person specification. But there are some instances when even religious and political affiliations have to be assessed (e.g. in selecting for a job in the Middle East, or for certain local authority appointments).

Availability can, therefore, refer to ability to fit in with hours of work, or to travel/spend time away from home, or to relocate, or to be likely to be granted a work permit. Continental shiftwork, for example, is not everybody's cup of tea, and an employer arguably has the right to ask questions about a candidate's domestic commitments or social activities in relation to shiftwork.

Local commitments might also restrict a person's ability to travel or relocate. A candidate for a sales management post involving extensive UK travel was turned down because of his heavy involvement in local community activities. Heavy evening/weekend commitments to adult education and amateur football were considered likely to interfere with the need to travel extensively around his region (which his previous job had not required him to do). This may seem a little hard, but selection is always about reducing the risks of job failure. Another approach to this problem would be to ask the candidate whether they would be prepared to give up some of their outside activities if offered the job. Here we see a further example of the interrelatedness of the seven points – in this case, data about Interests were used to support a judgement about Circumstances. Indeed, there is some overlap between the two points – social or political involvement may be relevant (a) because it provides information about motivation and/or (b) because it might limit a person's availability or performance.

Candidates with elderly parents provide another example of the relevance of Circumstances. If a candidate has elderly, dependent relatives in poor health, they may feel a strong obligation to look after them and their ability to relocate may be limited. On the other hand, if there are other brothers or sisters living nearby who are able to do so, the problem may not arise. Questions about a candidate's family are not just idle curiosity!

There is some evidence to support these arguments. Factors such as distance from work have been shown to be related to job performance and turnover. There have been several studies of the 'weighted application form' technique, by which items on an application form which show a relationship to job criteria are given greater weight in the selection decision. PA Personnel Services' Biodata technique provides a detailed breakdown of characteristics which have been found to predict success in a particular job, from Circumstances and other areas. And there is certainly evidence to suggest that recruiters are influenced by such factors as area of permanent address and marriage status in screening applicants on the basis of their application forms. (Wingrove et al., 1984).[34]

The Seven Point Plan approach has come under attack in some quarters from those who consider questioning about present circumstances and even interests to be wrong. The argument is partly that an investigation of circumstances constitutes an invasion of privacy, but the main concern seems to be about indirect unfair discrimination. Indirect discrimination occurs when candidates from a particular ethnic or racial group, or of a particular sex, are treated differently from other candidates. Indirect discrimination is often unintentional. If female candidates with young children are asked about the arrangements which they intend to make for them to be looked after, but male candidates with young children are not, this constitutes indirect discrimination on grounds of gender.

Similarly, if ethnic minority candidates are asked questions about their family background which are not put to other candidates, indirect discrimination has occurred. The concept of unlawful indirect discrimination is spelt out in the Sex Discrimination Act (1975), the Race Relations Act (1976), and the Commission for Racial Equality's Code of Practice (1983).[35]

If there was such a clear-cut difference in the treatment of different groups in a selection procedure then indirect discrimination would undoubtedly have occurred. But the Seven Point Plan approach, correctly applied, would never lead to such an unintelligent policy. If availability is a key issue, all candidates should be asked questions about their family commitments. An interviewer should not assume that a male candidate has a wife who is going to stay at home and look after the children. Nor should the interviewer assume that a female candidate with children would be unable to cope.

Both assumptions are wrong because they are assumptions – one of the fundamental assessment errors identified earlier. Surely it is far better to encourage selection interviewers to establish the facts. If they are prevented from doing so they are more – not less – likely to play it safe and assume that a man is a better risk than a woman. The actual questions which are put to each candidate will always differ to some extent, because the information available to the interviewer from the application form will be different in each case and because each candidate's circumstances are unique!

The interviewer should always be able to justify a line of questioning in terms of the job requirements, but this is not difficult where Circumstances are concerned. An examination of personnel records in most organisations would show 'circumstantial' factors to be a major reason for leaving service. Sometimes people's circumstances change unpredictably, but in many cases a simple check at the selection stage would have identified the problem area which eventually led the employee to resign.

CIRCUMSTANCES

Early Background (past circumstances and their effects on the person's development)

> Place of birth
> Location(s) in childhood
> Family occupations and socio-economic level
> Effects of family mobility/stability
> Effects of parental expectation and attitudes
> Financial, cultural, emotional influences
> Domestic problems

Present Circumstances (factors which could affect availability or performance)

Mobility

distance from place of work (versus frequency of attendance/need to be quickly available)

ability to travel within UK/abroad/live abroad

ability to drive

ability/willingness to relocate; partner's attitude towards relocation; effects of relocation on children's education etc.

Dependent relatives

Financial commitments

Religious, social, political and other commitments

Any special openings available to the person?

References

1. FRASER, J.M. (1978). *Employment Interviewing*. London: Macdonald & Evans.

2. OLDFIELD, R.C. (1941). *The Psychology of the Interview*. London: Methuen.

3. MILLS, M.M. (1978). *Selection Interviewing Course Notes*. Kings Langley: Mills & Nuttall.

4. HIGHAM, M. (1979). *The ABC of Interviewing*. London: Institute of Personnel Management.

5. BOLTON, G.M. (1983). *Interviewing for Selection Decisions*. Windsor: NFER-NELSON.

6. BOLTON, G.M. (1983). *Testing in Selection Decisions*. Windsor: NFER-NELSON.

7. DOWNS, S. (1985). *Testing Trainability*. Windsor: NFER-NELSON.

8. HERRIOT, P. (1981). 'Towards an attributional theory of the selection interview', *Journal of Occupational Psychology*, vol. 54, no. 3, pp. 165-74.

9. HOLLINGWORTH, H.L. (1929). *Vocational psychology and character analysis*. New York: Appleton Century Crofts.

10. ULRICH, L. and TRUMBO, D. (1965). 'The selection interview since 1949', *Psychological Bulletin*, vol. 63, no. 2, pp. 100-16.

11. SHELDON, W.H. and STEVENS, S.S. (1942). *The Varieties of Temperament*. New York: Harper.

12. TYLER, L.E. (1956). *The Psychology of Human Differences* (2nd edn.). New York: Appleton Century Crofts.

13. FORBES, R.J. and JACKSON, P.R. (1980). 'Non-verbal behaviour and the outcome of selection interviews', *Journal of Occupational Psychology*, vol. 53, no. 1, pp. 65-72.

14. ELLIOTT, A.G.P. (1981). 'Sex and decision-making in the selection interview: a real-life study', *Journal of Occupational Psychology*, vol. 54, no. 4, pp. 265-74.

15. HONEY, P. (1984). 'Accents at Work', *Personnel Management*, January 1984. London: Institute of Personnel Management.

16. TULLAR, W.E., MULLINS, T.W. and CALDWELL, S.A. (1979). 'Effects of interview length and applicant quality on interview decision time', *Journal of Applied Psychology*, vol. 64, pp. 669-74.

17. VERNON, P.E. (1979). *Intelligence: Heredity and Environment*. San Francisco: W.H. Freeman.

18. NFER-NELSON (1985). Catalogue of Tests for Industry and Commerce. Windsor: NFER-NELSON.

19. GARRETT, H.E. (1946). 'A development theory of intelligence', *American Psychologist*, vol. 1, pp. 372-8.

20. THURSTONE, L.L. (1938). 'Primary mental abilities'. Psychometric Monographs, no. 1. Chicago: University Press.

21. BENNETT, G.K., SEASHORE, H.G. and WESMAN, A.G. (1974). *Manual for the Differential Aptitude Tests*. New York: Psychological Corporation.

22. BOYD, D.P. (1984). 'Type A behaviour, financial performance and organizational growth in small business firms', *Journal of Occupational Psychology*, vol..57, no. 2, pp. 137-40.

23. JENKINS, C.D. (1979). *Jenkins Activity Survey Manual*. New York: The Psychological Corporation.

24. ZAGAR, R., ARBIT, J., FALCONER, J. and FRIEDLAND, J. (1983). 'Vocational interests and personality', *Journal of Occupational Psychology*, vol. 56, no. 3, pp. 203-14.

25. HOLLAND, L.J. (1978). *Manual for the Vocational Preference Inventory*. California: Consulting Psychologists Press..

26. SAVILLE & HOLDSWORTH LTD (1984). *Introducing the OPQ*. Esher: Saville & Holdsworth.

27. MYERS, I. (1962). *Manual for the Myers-Briggs Type Indicator*. California: Consulting Psychologists Press.

28. KIRTON, M.J. (1984). 'Adaptors and Innovators - why new initiatives get blocked', *Long Range Planning*, vol. 17, no. 2, pp. 137-43.

29. CARNE, G.C. and KIRTON, M.J. (1982). 'Styles of creativity: test-score correlations between Kirton Adaption–Innovation Inventory and Myers-Briggs Type Indicator, *Psychological Reports*, vol. 50, pp. 31-6.

30. REDDIN, W.J. (1970). *Managerial Effectiveness*. London: McGraw-Hill.

31. SMITH, K.C.P. and APTER, M.J. (1975). *A Theory of Psychological Reversals*. Chippenham: Picton Publishing.

32. APTER, M.J. (1982). *The Experience of Motivation: The Theory of Psychological Reversals*. London: Academic Press.

33. MURGATROYD, S. 'The Nature of Telic Dominance'. In APTER, M.J., FONTANA, D. and MURGATROYD, S., (Eds). *Reversal Theory – Development and Applications*. Cardiff: University College Press. (In press).

34. WINGROVE, J., GLENDINNING, R. and HERRIOT, P. (1984). 'Graduate pre-selection – a research note', *Journal of Occupational Psychology*, vol. 57, no. 2, pp. 169-71.

35, COMMISSION FOR RACIAL EQUALITY (1983). Code of Practice (Race Relations). London: Commission for Racial Equality.

Index